FOREWORD

The Hymn Society of Great Britain and Ireland is delighted to welcome members from our sister societies to the 2015 International Hymn Conference in Cambridge. When lovers and students of hymnody get together there is always much to discuss, and the theme of our Conference, 'Hymns in Liturgy and Life', provides many opportunities for the study of why, when and how we use hymns and sacred songs in the liturgy. Hymnologists are always particularly interested in the contribution of individual people to this process, so, when we considering how best to commemorate this year's International Conference we decided to investigate hymnody in Cambridge itself. Cambridge has an international reputation for the carols from King's College, but there is also a great wealth of other hymnic material relating to people and places associated with the city and region.

This is why the HSGBI has produced this Occasional Paper on the hymns and carols of Cambridge. We are fortunate that among our members we have those with the expertise to explore and document the historical and contemporary aspects of hymnody in Cambridge, and the editors are indeed most grateful to our authors for their contributions. The scope is vast, encompassing the fertile relationships between university and town which have existed for centuries. For instance, we read that in the 1780s a Fellow of Jesus College, William Frend, who was also the incumbent of Madingley Church, started a Sunday School of some forty children. He introduced hymn singing which proved to be so popular that the children's parents came early to church and stayed after the service to hear them! 'Town' and 'gown' still co-exist and influence each other, and in our 2015 Conference we are using the facilities of local churches and college chapels for many of our festivals and events.

Our publication is, then, an attempt to map the hymnic scene in this part of the world. It deals with those individuals who have lived, worked, studied and worshipped here. Inevitably, there will be gaps in our account, but we hope that we have charted the important contribution of those people - authors, composers, organists, instrumentalists, singers, scholars, liturgists, editors, publishers, worship leaders and countless worshippers - who have helped to shape the story of hymnody in Cambridge.

If we needed an additional theme for our Conference it would surely be those immortal words of John Milton in 'At a Solemn Music', set so memorably by Hubert Parry. Milton was inspired by the worship in Christ's College Chapel where he studied from 1625-1632. In those days higher education was restricted to the privileged few – men only! Today, though, the sounds of the music of Cambridge can be appreciated at the touch of a button by millions round the world who seek to 'keep in tune with Heaven'. The influence of Cambridge hymns and carols has never been greater.

> O may we soon again renew that Song,
> And keep in tune with Heaven, till God ere long
> To his celestial consort us unite,
> To live with him, and sing in endless morn of light.

Ian Sharp
(Executive President of the Hymn Society
of Great Britain and Ireland)
July 2015

Cambridge Hymns and Carols:
Town and Gown in Liturgy and Life

Edited by Gordon Giles, Martin Leckebusch & Ian Sharp

Contents

Author Biographies

GORDON GILES

Gordon Giles holds degrees in Music and Aesthetics (Lancaster), Philosophy (Cambridge, M.Litt) and Liturgy and Hymnody (Middlesex, PhD). After ordination he served as curate at the Church of the Good Shepherd, Cambridge, was Succentor of St Paul's Cathedral, London, and is now Vicar of St Mary Magdalene, Enfield, in North London. He has written widely on hymns, liturgy and music, and is an editor of both *Ancient & Modern* (2013) and the forthcoming revision of the *English Hymnal*.

CHRISTOPHER IDLE

Christopher Idle's seventy-six years have included thirty in Anglican parish ministry (from inner-urban to remote rural) and forty married to Marjorie who died in 2003. His writing includes two collections of hymns and the two-part hymnal companion *Exploring Praise!*[1]. He has served on five hymn book editorial groups and is involved in the peace movement.

VALERIE RUDDLE

Valerie Ruddle is a graduate of the Royal Academy of Music and taught music in England and the West Indies. She is a Methodist lay preacher and has been Director of Music at Sevenoaks Methodist Church for about 25 years. She enjoys leading contemplative worship and workshops on developing musical talents. She has researched and written about the origins of many hymn tune names.

---

[1] Idle, Christopher, *Exploring Praise*, Praise Trust, Darlington, Volume 1, 2006; Volume 2, 2007

DAVID THOMPSON

David Thompson, a Past Moderator of the General Assembly of the URC and an ordained non-stipendiary minister, was Convener of the Editorial Committee for *Rejoice and Sing*. He holds a personal chair in modern church history at the University of Cambridge, where he has taught for over forty years and where he pioneered the teaching of world Christianity. He is a Fellow of the Royal Historical Society.

JANET WOOTTON

The Rev'd Dr Janet Wootton MA is Director of Studies for the Congregational Federation. Before taking up this post in 2003, she was minister of Congregational churches in rural and inner city settings for nearly 25 years. She is editor of *Worship Live*[2] and author of a number of books and worship resources. In 2014 she was elected Executive Vice-Chair of the Hymn Society.

MARTIN LECKEBUSCH

Martin Leckebusch is Co-ordinator of the HSGBI Publications Committee and the author of around five hundred hymns. As an Oxford Mathematics graduate who has worked in IT since leaving university, he has no qualifications to edit a booklet on Cambridge hymnody.

IAN SHARP

Ian Sharp, HSGBI Executive President, is an Emeritus Senior Fellow in Church Music at Liverpool Hope University where he taught Music and Education Studies, retiring in 2003 as Foundation Dean. He was educated at Lincoln College, Oxford and the universities of Birmingham, York and Liverpool (PhD). He is a Fellow and Choirmaster of the Royal College of Organists, an Honorary Fellow of the RSCM, and the composer of a number of hymn tunes.

---

[2] www.worshiplive.org.uk

PHIIP SPENCE (ILLUSTRATOR)

Philip Spence studied at the Burslem School of Art under the cartoonist J.W. Taylor and worked as a pottery artist with Royal Doulton Potteries. He was a Methodist minister for twelve years before retraining at Westcott House, Cambridge, and transferring to Church of England ministry. He was Vicar of St Mark's Church, Newnham and Honourary Chaplain of Wolfson College, Cambridge. In retirement, he illustrates books and magazines, and lectures on the lives and works of famous artists.

(Ralph Vaughan Williams by Philip Spence)

Abbreviations

A&M   *Hymns Ancient and Modern* (see Bibliography)

ABRSM   Associated Board of the Royal Schools of Music

ARCM   Associate of the Royal College of Musicians

ARCO   Associate of the Royal College of Organists

CAM   *The Cambridge Hymnal* (see Bibliography)

CCB   *The Cambridge Carol Book* (see Bibliography)

CFC(1-5) *Carols for Choirs*, Volumes 1-5

CUMS   Cambridge University Musical Society

EH   *The English Hymnal* (see Bibliography)

FRCO   Fellow of the Royal College of Organists

H&P   *Hymns & Psalms* (see Bibliography)

HSGBI   Hymn Society of Great Britain and Ireland

HSUSC   Hymn Society in the United States and Canada

HTC   *Hymns for Today's Church* (see Bibliography)

IAH   Internationale Arbeitsgemeinschaft für Hymnologie

LRAM   Licentiate of the Royal Academy of Music

NEB   *New English Bible*

NEH   *The New English Hymnal* (see Bibliography)

RAM   Royal Academy of Music

R&S   *Rejoice and Sing* (see Bibliography)

RCM   Royal College of Music

RSCM   Royal School of Church Music

URC   United Reformed Church

CAMBRIDGE CAROLS

Gordon Giles

The Cambridge Carol Book, 'being fifty-two songs for Christmas, Easter, and other seasons', reminds us that, while there grew a tendency in the twentieth century to call any Christmas hymn or song a 'carol', the term extends wider than that, encompassing other, and indeed, no seasonal flavours or focus. Such a scope is far too broad for our purposes, so this chapter is mostly concerned with Christmas hymns and songs that have obvious or obscure connections with the City, University or County of Cambridge.

Beginning with the Christmas material in *The Cambridge Carol Book*, I will move forward to consider the contributions made to the world of Christmastide by *The Cambridge Hymnal*, and the *Carols for Choirs* series, and will conclude with some comments on the world-famous phenomenon that is the 'Nine Lessons and Carols from King's'. These make up the three legs of Cambridge carolling, providing us with an historical context; a publishing phenomenon and a vehicle for the outpouring of a vein of compositional opportunity that is still very rich indeed.

I shall focus on both musicians and writers, drawing out particular 'Cambridge' connections and origins. It should be observed at the very outset though, that the world of carol singing would be nothing like what it is today were it not for the seminal influence of men and women such as G.R. Woodward, Elizabeth Poston, Sir David Willcocks and John Rutter; the Cambridge choral tradition which nurtured and sustained them, and the growth into the 'Carol Capital of the World' that Cambridge has become over the last century.

The Cambridge Carol Book

The Cambridge Carol Book (*CCB*) was published in 1924 by SPCK (and reprinted in 1951), with George Ratcliffe Woodward (1848-1934) having selected the words and Charles Wood (1866-1926) as the musical editor, although Woodward prepared some of the harmonies and **George Herbert Palmer** (1846-1926) did one. Palmer, coincidentally, had been born in Grantchester, very close to

1

Cambridge. He was educated at Trinity College, gaining his BA in 1868 and having being ordained very soon after, served as curate in Liverpool and then St Barnabas, Pimlico, before settling in Oxford. It was in Oxford that he got to know Woodward well.

A stronger Cambridge connection comes through **Charles Wood**, who became Professor of Music at Cambridge in 1924, having been a University Lecturer since 1897. Wood had come up to Cambridge in 1889 after transferring his Organ Scholarship at Selwyn to Gonville and Caius, where in 1894 he was elected Fellow of the College. Prior to that, between 1883-87, Wood had studied at the Royal College of Music, under fellow Irishman **Charles Villiers Stanford** (1852-1924). As well as being instrumental in the production of *The Cambridge Carol Book*, Wood had worked with Woodward on *Carols for Christmas-tide* (1892-93)[3], *The Cowley Carol Book* (1901 and 1919),[4] *Songs of Syon* (1904, reprinted 1910)[5] and *An Italian Carol Book* (1920).[6] *The Cambridge Carol Book* was therefore the culmination of three decades of collaborative work between the two men, involving Palmer too. While none of these publications have attained great fame or lasting impact, as a body of scholarship and enthusiasm they launched an interest in carols on which was founded all subsequent work. *The Oxford Book of Carols*[7], published in 1928 and edited by **Ralph Vaughan Williams** (1872-1958), **Percy Dearmer** (1867-1936) and **Martin Shaw** (1875-1958) who had been members of the team producing *The English Hymnal* of 1906, learned from and owed a great deal to the Wood / Woodward series of carol books.

The inheritance of the series that culminated with *The Cambridge Carol Book* can be traced back to the middle of the nineteenth century, to Woodward's association with **John Mason Neale** (1818-66) and **Thomas Helmore** (1811-90), who had served at St Barnabas, Pimlico (as had Palmer). **George Ratcliffe Woodward**

---

[3] Published by Pickering & Chatto, London
[4] Published by A.R. Mowbray & Company, London and Oxford
[5] Woodward, G.R., *Songs of Syon: A Collection of Hymns and Sacred Poems Mostly Translated from Ancient Greek, Latin and German Sources*, Schott (music) and Plainsong & Medieval Music Society (text)
[6] Wood, C. and Woodward, G.R., *An Italian Carol Book; being a selection of Laude Spirituali of the xvith and xviith centuries*, Faith Press, Leighton Buzzard, 1920
[7] Oxford University Press, Oxford

had been inspired by Neale's work and the tenets of the Oxford Movement while a student at Gonville and Caius, where he took his BA in 1872. Ordained in 1874, Woodward went to St Barnabas to serve his title, and after two years was instrumental in the appointment of Palmer as 'priest-organist'. Thus early friendships and associations were formed that extended backwards to Helmore and Neale and forwards to the series of carol books. Woodward worked with Palmer at St Barnabas, and they founded the Plainsong and Medieval Music Society in 1888, under whose auspices the early carol books were published. Meanwhile, Woodward and Wood were both alumni of Gonville and Caius College, albeit a decade apart.

The scene was therefore set for Woodward, Wood and Palmer to emulate the work of Helmore and Neale who had kick-started a Victorian interest in carols with their *Carols for Christmas-Tide*,[8] a volume of twelve carols, published in 1853. With it they had introduced *Piæ Cantiones* to the English-speaking world. Created by Theodoricus Petri in 1582, this contained 74 Latin songs, of which 24 were Christmas-themed. Neale and Helmore drew on this newly-discovered body of material to give us '*In Dulci Jubilo*' and 'Good King Wenceslas'. Woodward himself produced a new edition of the original collection for the Plainsong and Medieval Music Society in 1910: *Piæ Cantiones. A Collection of Church & School Song, chiefly Ancient Swedish, originally Published in A.D. 1582 by Theodoric Petri of Nyland.* By then Woodward had already produced *Carols for Christmas-Tide* (using the same title in tribute to Neale and Helmore), and had come into contact with Wood. In the 1897 preface to *Hymns and Carols for Christmas-tide*,[9] Woodward presented the background to his endeavour:

> So many Carols suitable for the sacred and joyful season of our Lord's Nativity are already in the field that the appearance of yet another volume seems to call for a word of explanation.
>
> Several years ago the late Rev. T. Helmore lent the Editor his copy of the "Piæ Cantiones," printed at

---

[8] Published by Novello, London
[9] Published by H. Grice, London

Greifswald in 1582. This was the source whence he and Dr. Neale derived the lovely melodies of their "Carols for Christmas-tide" and "Carols for Easter-tide," which collections published in 1853 and 1854, are, in the Editor's opinion, unquestionably far and away the best of all the Christmas and Easter carols that has yet appeared. It was evident, however, that the treasures of "Piæ Cantiones" were by no means exhausted; and as Dr. Neale was no longer amongst us, and as modern poets, seemingly, have a strong dislike to be fettered by the original metrics when translating from Latin or German into the English tongue, the Editor had no alternative but himself to essay translations. It seemed a pity that such beautiful words and tunes, e.g., as those of "Puer nobis nascitur" in "Piæ Cantiones" and of "Quem pastores laudavere," in German hymners, should remain for the most part unknown to English Churchmen.[10]

Woodward went on to explain his rationale, saying of the music:

> Though modern musicians may understand the laws of Harmony better than their predecessors, yet our forefathers undoubtedly possessed the art of writing lovely, flowing diatonic Melodies. The writers of these Carols were the contemporaries of the men who built Durham Cathedral and Westminster Abbey, who painted the windows in York Minster, and illuminated the manuscripts which we still see and admire at the British Museum.[11]

Such comments give an insight into Woodward's devotion to and passion for disseminating and improving ancient hymns and songs:

> ... if they find their way into the hearts of some, and help in any way to emphasize the doctrine of the

---

[10] Woodward, G.R., *Hymns and Carols for Christmas–tide*, H. Grice, London 1897, Preface (*sic*: Woodward has 'nascitus' and 'churchman'). See http://www.hymnsandcarolsofchristmas.com/Hymns_and_Carols/Notes_On_Carols/hymns_and_carols_for_christmas-tide_1897.htm#Preface, accessed 06/06/15.
[11] ibid. Woodward has "Durum Cathedral and Westminster Abby".

Incarnation of our Lord Jesus Christ and the mother Mary, and if they prove an aid to those who love to celebrate the Birthday of the Holy Child, then the Editors labor will be amply rewarded.[12]

The collection itself is rather eclectic, but merits attention, even if it has been dwarfed in every sense by the carol book which takes its name from the 'other place', *The Oxford Carol Book*. The Cambridge book does contain some gems, and is probably to be noted most for introducing to us the now ubiquitous 'Ding Dong! merrily on high' (No. 8). Undoubtedly the most famous of Woodward's carols, he wrote words for a tune which he sourced from the *Orchésographie* of 1588 by Thoinot Arbeau (1520-1595), whose real name was Jehan Tabourot. A priest who was in favour of dancing, his *Orchésographie* was the only dance manual published in France in the second half of the sixteenth century. It provides invaluable and unique information about the nature, style and performance practices of his age, although in it he provided only melodies, expecting harmonies to be improvised in execution. Wood harmonised the *'Branle de l'Official'*, with its extended setting of refrain Glorias and use of the expression of joy, 'io', which combine with the macaronic use of English and Latin to create a rather exotic mix:

And i-o, i-o, i-o
By priest and people sungen
Gloria, Hosanna in excelsis!

As well as 'Ding! Dong!', Woodward is to be credited with 'Past Three a clock', which is still very much in use. It is interesting to note at the outset that this carol has become known as 'Past Three O'clock', but should strictly be called, as Woodward indicated, 'Past Three a clock'. As Woodward himself put it: 'The refrain, *Past three a clock* is old, but the rest of the Carol is newly composed by George Ratcliffe Woodward. The tune (London Waits, from W. Chappell's *Popular Music of the Olden Time*, p.550) is here harmonised by Charles Wood.'[13] The words of the refrain had

---

[12] ibid.
[13] *CCB*, p.27.

appeared in John Playford's *Dancing Master*,[14] and were often quoted in the eighteenth and nineteenth centuries:

Past three a clock,
And a cold frosty morning,
Past three a clock;
Good morrow, masters all!

One of the tasks of the City Waits was to call out the hours during the night, and this carol is probably derived from a call of the London City Waits, greeting the beginning of the morning (although 3am does seem uncivilly early to rise!). Modern versions and arrangements are still in use, including this very version found as No. 31 in *Carols for Choirs 1*; and another version arranged by John Rutter in *Carols for Choirs 2*, No. 32. The juxtaposition of the waits' early morning cry with verses about the Christmas story is a little unusual, and Woodward's characteristic use of archaisms makes the carol appear more authentic than it is. The similarities with 'Ding Dong!' are striking in this respect. Some of the verses are quirky for sure: the idea of bringing milk from the dairy for Mary, and honey for no money, seems contrived in the extreme, even if one might surmise a reference to the promised land flowing with milk and honey from Exodus 3:8. Another verse of Woodward's refers not to Kings nor Magi nor Wise Men nor Sages, but to 'princes' who 'worship and greet him'. Ultimately the carol does what Woodward tried to do in almost all of his work: blend a quaint, homely understanding of Christmas goodwill with the nativity story, making it not just homely, but bringing it into the home, so that it should be taken into the heart, inspiring those who sing truly to 'own' the story and the deeper meaning it conveys. There are many reasons why so much of his material has now sunk without trace, but the strength of the jaunty tune of 'Past Three a clock' and its selection by Willcocks and Jacques forty years after Woodward wrote it have given this carol, at least, a place that will last in the Christmas repertoire. Arguably it is neither better nor worse than many of Woodward's others, but as is often the case with hymnody, it is not necessarily the best examples of an author's work that

---

[14] 3rd edition, 1665

become ubiquitous, but those which capture the imagination of the people who have the power to publish and set the trends.

Another carol in the book has a deeper Cambridge connection worth mentioning. 'Get Ivy and Hull, Woman, Deck up' (No. 10) is a text not by Woodward but by the sixteenth-century poet **Thomas Tusser** (c.1524-80), which was paired by Charles Wood with his own harmonization of 'Bannocks o' barley meal', a Scottish jig, the source of which was probably No. 25 in *White's Unique Collection* (1896). Wood transposed it down from D to G. The text was published by the American scholar Edith Rickert in her *Ancient English Christmas Carols: 1400-1700* in 1914.[15] A refrain appears at the end of each verse in the CCB, which Rickert only inserted after the first verse:

> At Christmas be merry and thank God of all,
> And feast thy poor neighbours, the great and the small.
> Yea, all the year long have an eye to the poor,
> And God shall send luck to keep open thy door.

Woodward and Wood printed it twice (to fit the tune), and added the same final two lines that Rickert had included:

> For plants and for stocks lay aforehand to cast,
> But set or remove them, while Twelve-tide do last.

An even earlier version of the carol appeared in Henry Vizetelly's *Christmas With The Poets,* published in 1851, in which the first verse is slightly different, and has no sequel. The author, Tusser, has Cambridge connections of his own. Born in Rivenhall, Essex, he was a chorister at Wallingford Castle, Oxfordshire, but it seems he declined to sing at the King's Chapel, preferring to join the choir of St. Paul's Cathedral, after which he went to Eton College. In 1543, when he must have been at least twenty, he was elected to King's College, Cambridge but moved to Trinity Hall, Cambridge. After his studies he went as court musician to serve William, 1st Baron Paget of Beaudesart for ten years. Then around 1560 he married and settled as a farmer in Cattawade in Suffolk, having

---

[15] Rickert, Edith, *Ancient English Christmas Carols: 1400-1700*, Chatto & Windus, London, 1914, p.225.

published, in 1557, *Hundred Good Pointes of Husbandrie.* He moved to West Dereham, Norfolk, and then to Norwich where he became a Lay-clerk at Norwich Cathedral. In 1572 he moved to London and lived near St Giles's, Cripplegate until the plague struck, at which point he returned to Cambridge, where he matriculated at Trinity College on 5th December, 1573, probably as a member of the choir. However, he ended his days in a debtors' prison near Poultry (Cheapside), London, died on 3rd May, 1580 and was buried in St Mildred's Church, Poultry.[16] The church, destroyed in the Great Fire of 1666, was rebuilt by Wren, but demolished in 1872.

A carol over which Woodward took some care and which has survived to some extent appeared as No. 15, 'Hob & Colin, Yule is come'. He based his text on an old Burgundian carol entitled '*Guillô, pran ton tamborin*' (based on the air, '*Ma mere mariez-moi*', ('My mother, marry me'), written by **Bernard de la Monnoye** (1641-1728). Wood arranged the music, accompanying words which Woodward based on those of the ancient Burgundian carol. The original text ran:

Guillô, pran ton tamborin;	William, take your drum,
Toi, pran tai fleúte, Rôbin!	You, take your flute, Robin!
Au son de cé instruman,	To the sound of these instruments
Turelurelu, patapatapan,	Tu-re-lu-re-lu, pata-pata-pan,
Au son de cé instruman	To the sound of these instruments
Je diron Noei gaiman.	I will say Christmas cheerfully.

Other versions of the carol have become known as 'Patapan' including a popular modern version by Reginald Jacques (1894-1969)[17] in *Carols for Choirs 2,* and a version translated by 'O.B.C.'

---

[16]For details see
http://venn.lib.cam.ac.uk/cgi-bin/search.pl?sur=&suro=c&fir=&firo=c&cit=
&cito=c&c=all&tex=%22TSR543T%22&sye=&eye=&col=all&maxcount=50,
accessed 11/01/15
[17] See Willcocks, D and Rutter J, *Carols for Choirs 2*, Oxford University Press, Oxford, 1970, No. 49, p.212 and Dearmer, P, Shaw, M and Vaughan Williams, R,

(i.e. the editors) in the *Oxford Book of Carols*, in 1928. Although he introduced the carol to the English-speaking world, Woodward's adventurous text is the weakest compared with the versions surviving through the Oxford tradition which are briefer and do not preserve Woodward's quaintness. Nevertheless, the Cambridge version is a key stepping stone on the journey of this carol, which was discovered in an edition of Bernard de la Monnoye's poems entitled *Noëls Bourgignons de Bernard de la Monnoye* published in 1842 by F. Fertiault. Monnoye had been born in Dijon and moved to Paris in later life, where he became a well-known poet, sometimes publishing under the pseudonym of Gui Barozai. *Noei borguignon* (Burgundian Christmas) was a collection of thirteen carols published in 1700, and later that year he published a further sixteen in *Noei tô nôvea*. Woodward probably sourced the carol from William Sandys' *Christmas Carols Ancient and Modern* or *Christmas-tide, Its History, Festivities and Carols, With Their Music*.[18] He had previously published it a year earlier in *The Babe Of Bethlehem, Being Some Christmas Carols*.[19] Only two hundred copies were made, containing only texts. Sandys was a well known antiquary and collector, a contemporary of Charles Dickens (1812-70), who along with him set in motion a thrust towards a distinctive type of Christmas celebratory culture that persists today. Woodward pursued this direction, furthering both Dickens' sentimentality and Sandys' academic research. This is why Woodward is to be recognized as a significant contributor to the study and promulgation of the Christmas carol repertoire, without actually being valued highly for many of his individual offerings, few of which have survived in popular use.

Consequently much of the *CCB*'s contents are, sadly but justifiably, neglected. In total it contained fifty-three carols, of which the first thirty-four are classified as Christmas Carols. Nowadays we are effectively left with 'Ding Dong!', 'The Linden Tree Carol' (classified

---

The Oxford Book of Carols, Oxford University Press , Oxford, rev edition, 1964, No. 82, p.177.

[18] See Sandys, William, *Christmas Carols Ancient and Modern*, Richard Beckley, London, 1833, and Sandys, William, *Christmas-tide, Its History, Festivities and Carols, With Their Music* John Russell Smith, London, 1852, pp. 279-80.

[19] *The Babe Of Bethlehem, Being Some Christmas Carols* published by GRW, at 48 West Hill, Highgate Village, 1923, No.18.

as a Lady Day Carol by Woodward), and 'Past Three a clock', (the three of which found their way into *Carols for Choirs 1*) and 'While shepherds watched' from this collection, but Woodward can hardly claim the credit for that one. The remaining half of the book contains material very much in keeping with the Christmas section, and none of its items have found a footing in popular hymnody. Woodward's penchant for archaisms have not endeared him to his successors, but there can be no mistake that the *CCB* paved the way for later books and anthologies and laid some of the foundations for what may justifiably be called the Cambridge Carol Tradition.

Carols in *The Cambridge Hymnal*

One successor to *CCB* that should not go unnoted is *The Cambridge Hymnal*, which appeared in 1967[20]. With texts edited by David Holbrook and music edited by Elizabeth Poston, it has a significant final section of Christmas hymns and carols. **David Holbrook** (1923-2011) was a student at Downing whose academic career was interrupted by the Normandy Campaign. Completing his degree in 1947, he taught at Bassingbourne Village College, later becoming a Fellow of both King's and Downing Colleges. As an educationalist he was committed to hymn-singing in schools and believed that many children were not really aware of the meaning of what they were singing. With *The Cambridge Hymnal* (*CAM*) he intended to address this issue, working with Poston (who lived in Stevenage) to provide material that drew on folk songs and other accessible material.

Elizabeth Poston (1905-87) was a fine musician who had trained at the Royal Academy of Music as a pianist and composer. She worked for the BBC for two decades before devoting herself to the collection of carols in the 1960s. In 1965 she published *The Penguin Book of Christmas Carols*, a second volume of which appeared five years later. [21] In between she collaborated with Holbrook on *CAM*, which had begun as an idea to revise *The*

---

[20] For further discussion of *CAM* see the article by Idle, Christopher, "The Living Tradition".

[21] Poston, Elizabeth, *The Penguin Book of Christmas Carols*, Penguin, London, 1965; *The Second Penguin Book of Christmas Carols*, Penguin, London, 1970

English Hymnal (a task eventually undertaken in 1987), a project she had discussed with Vaughan Williams himself.

The provision of carols in *CAM* might even be thought disproportionate. Hymns numbered 1-138 are general, or relate to other seasons, such as Passiontide or Easter, and the Christmas Section contains forty carols (numbers 140-180). A few familiar favourites are included: 'The First Nowell', 'God rest you merry', 'Hark! The Herald', 'In the bleak mid-winter', *'Adeste Fideles'* (in both Latin and English), 'While Shepherds watched' and The Sussex Carol, but all of the others are more esoteric, novel, and by now, forgotten or passed over. Nevertheless there is a real sense in which Poston took forward Woodward's enthusiasm and in *CAM* introduced some significant contributions to the public. That *CAM* was not a publishing success is a shame, not least for its Christmas provision.

The first of the carols is a now-forgotten setting of 'Adam Lay ybounden' commissioned especially from **Norman Fulton** (1909-80). Unlike many choral versions now in use, notably that by Boris Ord, this version was intended for unison and therefore congregational singing. Fulton also contributed 'The Chanticleer's Carol', setting a text which originated with William Austin of Lincoln's Inn Fields (1587-1633), printed in *A Handfull of Celestial Flowers*, written out by Ralph Crane in *Ancient Christmas Carols*, edited by Edith Rickert in 1910.[22] The first verse ran:

> All this night shrill chanticleer,
> Day's proclaiming trumpeter,

---

[22] See Rickert, Edith, *Ancient English Christmas Carols: 1400-1700*, Chatto & Windus, London, 1914, pp.200-201.

Claps his wings and loudly cries,
'Mortals, mortals, wake and rise!
    See a wonder
    Heaven is under,
From the earth is risen a Sun
Shines all night though day be done

The composer **Nicholas Maw** (1935-2009) had lectured in the Music Faculty at Cambridge, and he was asked to arrange Ralph Vaughan Williams' 'Corpus Christi Carol', a carol from Derbyshire which only makes its Christmas credentials clear in the final stanza:

Over that bed the moon shines bright:
    The bells of Paradise I heard them ring:
Denoting our Saviour was born this night:
    And I love my Lord Jesus above anything.

Vaughan Williams' 'The Blessed Son of God' extracted from his *Hodie* was also included, and still survives in modern use. The text is a paraphrase of Luther by **Miles (Myles) Coverdale** (1487-1568), who gained a Cambridge degree in Canon Law in 1513 before joining the Austin Friars where he probably came into contact with the Cambridge martyr Robert Barnes (c.1495-1540). As a Bible Translator, thinker, theologian and poet, Coverdale's influence on the spiritual and literary history of the English speaking world cannot be overestimated, nor his Cambridge connection overlooked.

Benjamin Britten (1913-78), who had Suffolk rather than Cambridge connections, made a lovely arrangement of 'The Holly and the Ivy', and **Stanley Taylor** (b.1902) wrote a setting of Isaac Watts' 'Hush my dear, lie still and slumber'. He also arranged 'Sweet was the song' (Virgin's Lullaby) especially for *CAM*, and his 'New Year Carol' was also included.

Another commission, Lennox Berkeley's 'I sing of a Maiden' appeared for the first time, although he was very much an Oxford man who had much admired and lived with Britten in the 1930's. Christopher Morris (b.1922) was commissioned to write 'In a field as I lay', a fourteenth-century carol. Peter Warlock's 'Where riches is everlastingly', ('Into this world this day did come Jesus Christ, both God and man'), with text by Ben Jonson was also included.

Alan Ridout's 'Lullay, lullay, thou lytil child' drew its text from an anonymous manuscript in the Cambridge University library. Like Maw, Ridout (1934-96) had lectured in the faculty (although he spent most of his life in Canterbury and ultimately moved to France). 'Nowell, nowell, nowell' by **Elizabeth Machonchy** (1907-94) was also new for the book, and used a late fifteenth century text from a manuscript in Trinity College Library, printed in *Musica Britannica* which had been edited by Professor John Stevens of Magdalene. His 'There is no rose' was included in two versions and survived to be included in the *Carols for Choirs* series. He wrote a performance note on the second version of the carol, explaining that the accidentals could be ignored and pointing out that the tune is in the tenor (Burden).

From a Latin carol written by the Nuns of Chester c.1425, '*Qui creavit coelum*' by **Anthony Milner** (1925-2002) was also specially commissioned, and used the mixolydian mode as its harmonic basis. This contains a final line which is to be spoken: 'Puer natus est nobis!' ('The child is born for us!'). Gustav Holst's 'In the Bleak Midwinter' was included, and so too was his daughter Imogen's 'That Lord that lay in Assë stall'. Neither are associated with Cambridgeshire, and even the text of this carol was sourced at the Bodleian Library in Oxford.

The final carol in *CAM* was 'Twelfth Night Song', another new commission by Elizabeth Machonchy, a two-part unaccompanied song with a concluding four-part round. The text was by the poet **Robert Herrick** (1591-1674), taken from his *Hesperides*, and is all about changing the leafy decorations at the end of the Christmas season. The first verse ran:

> Down with the rosemary and bays,
> Down with the mistletoe;
> Instead of holly now upraise
> The greener box for show.

Poston may have made a mistake attributing the change of décor and relaxation of festivities to Twelfth Night, for it was customary to continue for the forty days until Candlemas (February 2nd), and the poem implies this. Herrick had matriculated at St John's College, Cambridge, at twenty-two, but moved to Trinity Hall in 1616, graduating the following year. He spent most of his life as Vicar of Dean Prior, in Devon, being both ejected from and restored to the living during and after the Civil War.

Poston herself made arrangements of 'A Virgin most pure', 'Behold a silly tender babe', 'The Boar's Head Carol', 'The first Nowell', 'God rest you merry', 'Hark the herald', 'Poor little Jesus', 'Jesus was born in Beth'ny' (A Virginian carol), 'Balulalow', 'Adeste Fideles' (for which she wrote a descant, which was to be supplanted by Willcocks'), 'Sing all men' (A Kentucky carol), 'The Virgin Mary had a baby boy', 'This endris night', 'Tomorrow shall be my dancing day' (unaccompanied and accompanied versions) and 'What tidings bring'st us, messenger' (with a text by John Audelay from the Library at Trinity). The carol 'Christmas Day' was actually written by Poston, to a text by Andrew Young. It has fallen into oblivion, not least because of the archaic strangeness of the text, so like so many that Woodward used in *CCB*. Poston's lasting contribution probably consists in the ever popular 'Jesus Christ the apple tree', a delicious carol which still bears much fruit today. The text first appeared in the *Spiritual Magazine* (London, August 1761), attributed to the now unknown contributor or author "R.H.", although the text may have earlier Methodist precursors. It was first published in a hymnal in America in 1784, giving rise to the spurious claim that it is an American hymn.

The carols in *CAM*, now looked at half a century later, remind us of the wealth of poor or obscure material that both CCB and *CAM* placed into the hands of any who would celebrate Christmas musically. Some of their work has survived, but is best noted, acknowledged and revered as key stepping stones on the journey to the now ubiquitous *Carols for Choirs* (*CFC*) provisions, which owe a great but often unseen debt to Woodward, Wood and Poston, even if very little of their material actually found its way into those subsequent volumes. It is worth remembering that the first *CFC* was published six years before *CAM*, and that the 'Festival of Nine Lessons and Carols' from King's was already well-established. *CAM* rode its own path when it came to carols, and never made anything like the impact that Willcocks and Rutter were to do only three years later with *CFC2*.

Carols for Choirs

The next major development in the 'Cambridge' Carol tradition was the publication in 1970 of the second volume of *Carols for Choirs*. What became known as Volume 1 had appeared in 1961, setting a standard which prevails today. Published by OUP in Oxford, there is a sense in which they seem to follow in the tradition of the *CCB*, but it should be noted, with irony perhaps, that the *CFC* books are more 'Cambridge' than 'Oxford'. While a book could be devoted in commentary upon them, it is worth remembering that David Willcocks and John Rutter are both thoroughly Cambridge men whose contribution to the carol-singing world is surely incalculable. This huge contribution to carol-singing and its repertoire comes through the inexorable connection made between the 'Carols from King's' performance tradition and the widespread adoption of these publications for choirs.

Sir **David Willcocks** (b.1919) began his musical career as a chorister at Westminster Abbey at the age of ten. At fourteen he left for Clifton College in Bristol, before becoming organ scholar at King's College, Cambridge, in 1939, studying under Boris Ord. War intervened and he served in the infantry, earning a Military Cross in 1944. He returned to his studies in 1945, and only two years later was made a Fellow of the College. The same year he became conductor of the Cambridge Philharmonic Society, conductor of the

Salisbury Musical Society and organist at Salisbury Cathedral. In 1950, he was appointed organist of Worcester Cathedral. After seven years he returned to Cambridge, succeeding Ord as Director of Music at King's, a post in which he remained until 1973, when he became Director of the Royal College of Music in London. In 1960 he had become Director of the Bach Choir, conducting them for thirty-eight years until 1988. He had succeeded Reginald Jacques (organist of Queen's College, Oxford), with whom he had collaborated on the first *Carols for Choirs* (1961). Now the doyen of the English choral world, Sir David retired to Cambridge. He was awarded a CBE in 1971.

John Rutter was born in London in 1945 and educated at Highgate School, before going to Clare College, where he displayed and developed early talent for composition, writing both words and music of the now ubiquitous 'Nativity Carol' and the 'Shepherd's Pipe Carol'. Delightful, even a little naïve in character, they express an excitement with the Christmas story, and set Rutter on path of popular appeal and success. While the accessibility of his early work established a pattern, one should not overlook his serious achievements as a Director of Clare College Choir between 1975 and 1979, and thereafter as Director of the world-renowned Cambridge Singers. As well as carols and short anthems (among them 'The Gaelic Blessing' and 'For the Beauty of the Earth'), he has written larger choral works, 'Gloria' (1974), 'Requiem' (1985), 'Magnificat' (1990), 'Psalmfest' (1993) and 'Mass of the Children' (2003), as well as orchestral music, some of which pays homage not only to the baroque but also to the Beatles. Rutter is also a highly accomplished editor of music, having not only co-edited Volumes 2-4 in the *CFC* series with Sir David Willcocks, but more recently edited the first two volumes in the new Oxford Choral Classics series, *Opera Choruses*[23] and *European Sacred Music*.[24] Rutter was awarded a CBE in 2007.

---

[23] Rutter, John (Ed.), *Opera Choruses*, Oxford University Press, Oxford, 1995
[24] Rutter, John (Ed.), *European Sacred Music*, Oxford University Press, Oxford, 1996

CAROLS FOR CHOIRS 1

Published in 1961, *CFC1* was effectively the carol book of King's College, Cambridge, and contains many arrangements of well-known Christmas hymns, with descants that have become as familiar as the carols themselves. *CFC1* also provided as an appendix the Bidding Prayers, the readings and the dismissal collect and blessing for the Nine Lessons and Carols, thereby inserting that liturgy into the heart of the English-speaking Christmas season. The seminal nature of this book cannot be overestimated: it trumped and superseded its predecessors, casting the *CCB* into oblivion and cementing the status of *The Oxford Book of Carols* as a reference work, rather than a practical book. Yet in this much *CFC1*, which had no successors in immediate vision, was insufficient. It contained very little 'modern' material, and stated in the editors' introductory note that 'Many of the carols are from traditional sources and include a number of well-loved tunes', and that they had been 'chosen and arranged with carol concerts and carol services in mind'.[25] The subtle distinction between a carol concert and a carol service was now official, and a trend set that is now widespread. Like Masses and Requiems before them, the Christmas Carol had entered the realm of entertainment. Similarly, the accompanying 'congre-gation / audience' leaflet for their use also provided for such a catholicity of use.

Wood and Woodward's 'Ding, Dong!' made it into *CFC1*, securing the survival of just one of their carols from *CCB*. Some Vaughan Williams, Britten and Walton material appeared, as did Joubert's 'Torches' and the 'Zither Carol' arranged by Sir Malcolm Sargent. Only four carols were brand new: 'O men from the fields' by **Arnold Cooke** (who had been educated at Gonville and Caius, and did a stint as Musical Director of the Festival Theatre at Cambridge); Reginald Jacques' 'When Christ was born' (which has antiquated fifteenth century words worthy of the *CCB*); Phyllis Tate's 'Carol, with Lullaby'; and William Walton's 'What Cheer'. While one can be sure that every church choir in the country still has copies of *CFC1*

---

[25] Jacques, Reginald and Willcocks, David, *Carols for Choirs*, Oxford University Press, Oxford, 1961, p.iii

in their vestries, it is also true that these four carols hardly ever find their way into the 'Nine Lessons' these days.

CAROLS FOR CHOIRS 2

It was to take another nine years[26] for the longed-for successor to *CFC1* to appear. By then Jacques had died, and his place had been taken by the young Rutter, whose 'Nativity' and 'Shepherd's Pipe' carols were included. Rutter also made half a dozen arrangements of other carols. Willcocks made ten, and included his old mentor Boris Ord's 'Adam Lay Ybounden'. In total there were fifty carols, some of which the editors described as 'secular', to meet the 'needs' of carol concerts given by choral societies. Orchestral accompaniments became available as *CFC2* made further inroads into the concert hall. Meanwhile the editors claimed that their offerings suited the 'average choir'.[27]

A further development was recognized, reflecting the books' Oxbridge heritage: Advent carol services have also grown in popularity, notably in schools and colleges where it is not possible to celebrate Christmas during term-time, but no generally accepted form of service has hitherto existed.[28] Again history was to be made, and the modern Advent Carol Service tradition can be traced to the provision in *CFC2* of the Order of Service provided by the Rev'd David Edwards (b.1929, Dean of King's 1966-70). Palestrina's 'Matin Responsory' and other Advent carols were included accordingly. Where *CFC1* resourced Christmas, *CFC2* began to resource Advent.

Thus the provision in *CFC2* was much wider and deeper in scope than its predecessor. In an appendix, two straightforward versions (i.e. without descants) of 'O come, all ye faithful' and 'Hark! The herald angels sing' were included to complement the versions in *CFC1*. New com-positions by Walton, William Mathias, Richard Rodney Bennett and Britten were included. The latter's 'A New Year Carol' extended the duration of the book, now carrying material from Advent to New Year, and providing a strong

---

[26] The editors say the gap was 'ten years' in their Preface.
[27] *Carols for Choirs 2*, Oxford University Press, Oxford, 1970, p.ii.
[28] ibid.

companion-volume to its predecessor, equipping church, school, college and cathedral choirs and choral societies with everything necessary for Christmas celebrations.

Patrick Hadley (1899-1973) wrote 'I sing of a Maiden' in 1936 and it was included in *CFC2*. Born in Cambridge, where his father was a Fellow (and later Master) of Pembroke College, Hadley himself went to Pembroke after the First World War and studied with Charles Wood. In 1938 he was elected to a Fellowship at Gonville and Caius and became as a lecturer in the music faculty. During World War II he covered for Boris Ord as Director of the Cambridge University Music Society (CUMS). After the war, in 1946 he was elected to the Chair of Music at Cambridge University, remaining Professor until his retirement in 1962.

Boris (Bernhard) **Ord** (1897-1961) had a tremendous influence on the Cambridge carol tradition, but never saw the fruition of the CFC books. Revered by Willcocks, he was, like him, schooled at Clifton College, and became organist and choirmaster of King's College, Cambridge, in 1929. He retired in 1957 (and was succeeded by Willcocks), his service only having been interrupted by the Second World War during which he served in the Royal Air Force (Harold Darke (1888-1976) covered during that period). Born at Clifton, Bristol, he died in Cambridge.

John Stevens (1921–2002), Fellow of Magdalene College and Professor of Professor of Medieval and Renaissance English, was also a keen musician, and his arrangement of 'There is no rose' was included in *CFC2*. Stevens had studied at Christ's Hospital school and gained a scholarship to Magdalene, where he spent his whole academic career, as Bye-Fellow (1948-50), Research Fellow (1950-53); Fellow (1953-88), Tutor (1958-74), President (1983-88); University Lecturer in English (1954-74), Reader in English and Musical History (1974-78) and Professor of Medieval and Renaissance English (1978-88). He was appointed FBA in 1975 and awarded a CBE in 1980. Between 1988 and 1995 he was Chairman of the Plainsong and Medieval Music Society. This author knew and played mediaeval music with him in the late 1980's and early 1990's when after his retirement he maintained strong links with the college and its Music Society.

CAROLS FOR CHOIRS 3

CFC3 appeared in 1978, and by it Willcocks and Rutter added another fifty carols to the by then well-established collection. Two specially commissioned carols were included, as well as other 'modern' carols by Richard Rodney Bennett, Britten, Holst and Mathias. One of the new carols was 'Tryste Noel' by Herbert Howells (1892-1983), dedicated to 'David and John' - Willcocks and Rutter respectively. Written in signature Howells style, it sets a text by the American poet Louise Imogen Guiney (1861-1920). The other new work was 'King Herod and the Cock' ('There was a star in David's land') by William Walton (1902-83). Willcocks and Rutter had several of their own pieces included, among them Willcocks' own 'Birthday Carol' ('Rejoice today with one accord') which he had written a few years previously for the Bach Choir. Willcocks' arrangements were of the 'Boar's Head Carol'; 'Christ was born on Christmas Day'; 'Come all ye worthy gentlemen'; 'Deck the hall'; 'Angelus ad Virginem'; 'He smiles within his cradle' (an Austrian carol); 'What child is this?'; 'Shepherds in the fields abiding' (words by G.R. Woodward); 'Gabriel's Message' (from the Basque); 'Il est né le divin enfant' (arranged for the King's Singers); and 'We three kings'. Willcocks' arrangement of this and 'Earth has many a noble city' took the content very firmly into Epiphany territory. Similarly, his arrangement of 'Lo! He comes with clouds descending' encompassed Advent. Furthermore, 'This Joyful Eastertide' by Wood and Woodward carried the book into Eastertide, albeit in an Appendix.

Rutter's 'Star Carol', 'Donkey Carol', 'Jesus Child' and 'Cradle Song' (based on a Flemish tune) appeared in CFC3, and his arrangements of other carols were 'A little child on the earth has been born' (Flemish Carol); 'Child in a manger'; 'Angel Tidings' (an arrangement of a Moravian carol); 'Wexford Carol' (an arrangement of an Irish Carol); 'In Dulci Jubilo'; and 'King Jesus hath a garden' (a Dutch carol).

English Literature Professor John Stevens of Magdalene was again represented with his arrangement of 'Sing we to this merry company'. At the end of the book was printed a useful if brief list of suggested non-Biblical poems, including poetry by Betjeman, Milton, Ryman and Southwell. Such a provision is very much in keeping with the King's College practice of including poetry as well as carols, hymns and readings in the televised 'Carols from King's' service (which is not identical with the 'Festival of Nine Lessons and Carols' model).

CAROLS FOR CHOIRS 4

The fourth volume in the series, which contained no preface, was specifically intended for choirs without men. On the back cover it stated its aims, which were to provide arrangements of the staple diet of Christmas for upper voices, both classic carols and some new arrangements. At the end of the book the Order of Service for a 'Nine Lessons and Carols' service was again included. Thus this book provided a complete manual for choirs without tenors or bases to 'do' Christmas. While one might lament the fact that some choirs cannot resource themselves in four parts, this recognition on Willcocks' and Rutter's part is commendable and provided a real resource. The usual suspects are included, with almost everything in the book being either arranged or written by Willcocks or Rutter. In the latter's case, he also rearranged his own popular carols, 'Nativity Carol', 'Donkey Carol' and 'Shepherd's Pipe Carol', among them. Unusually, the arrangement of the 'Star Carol' was not done by Rutter himself, but by Kenneth Pont, who has made several briefer or easier arrangements of Rutter's carols for OUP. One carol with some Cambridge heritage to notice is Rutter's arrangement of 'Hail! Blessed Virgin Mary', which was taken from Woodward and Wood's *Italian Carol Book* of 1920. One of the few items to be authentically for upper voices is 'There is no rose', lifted from Britten's *A Ceremony of Carols*.

The contribution of *CFC4* to the repertoire is therefore not so much specific as generic. It was a godsend for upper voice choirs, but provided little new for anyone else, and in this much has often been overlooked or ignored. Until *CFC5* was published, most choral singers (and especially the men!) would have hardly noticed its existence. Nevertheless it has a very important place in the Christmas repertoire, and being edited by Willcocks and Rutter, containing arrangements almost exclusively by themselves, it is the most thoroughly 'Cambridge' volume of carols there is.

100 CAROLS FOR CHOIRS

In 1987 a slightly different volume, *100 Carols for Choirs*, was published as a kind of double-length 'best hits' carol book. It contained a hundred carols, seventy-four from the *CFC* provision preceding it and twenty-six new ones, serving Advent, Christmas, Epiphany, and Easter seasons. Again the order of service for a Festival of Nine Lessons and Carols was included.

CAROLS FOR CHOIRS 5

The latest volume (2011) of *Carols for Choirs* was edited by Bob Chilcott (b.1955) and David Blackwell. **Bob Chilcott** was a chorister in King's College Choir under Sir David Willcocks and later a choral scholar who has kept strong connections with the choir and college. David Blackwell, Director of Music Publishing at OUP, and previously at the Associated Board of the Royal Schools of Music (ABRSM), has no Cambridge connections to speak of. Prepared in celebration of the fiftieth anniversary of *CFC1*, its editors thank 'Reginald Jacques, Sir David Willcocks and John Rutter, whose inspirational work has enabled the *CFC* series to take flight, and given us the energy to carry it forward with confidence'.[29] They had already written that the series was 'one of the most important Christmas resources for choir singers and conductors worldwide',[30] and pointed out that the series had given an impetus and opportunity to composers to write new carols. Thus *CFC5* is mainly made up of new material. With the contents page (which follows the tradition set in the previous books of listing carols by both their titles and their first lines) is a list suggesting which carols are suitable for seasons 'other than Christmas'.[31] Many of the carols are also published with orchestral parts which can be hired, just as many in *CFC1* and *CFC2* were and still can be.

Rutter's 'New Year', written to commemorate the 80th birthday of Her Majesty the Queen, is included, as is his 'Candlelight Carol'. **Malcolm Archer** (b.1952) was Organ Scholar at Jesus College,

---

[29] Chilcott, Bob and Blackwell, David, *Carols for Choirs 5*, Oxford University Press, Oxford, 2011, p.v.
[30] ibid.
[31] ibid., p.vii

Cambridge, in the early 1970's, and is represented by 'A little child there is yborn'. He went on to serve at Bristol, Wells and St Paul's Cathedrals before taking up a post at Winchester School which he currently holds. Francis Pott (b.1957) studied at Magdalene, under Hugh Wood and Robin Holloway, and would have undoubtedly come into contact with John Stevens. His new carol 'Mary laid her child among the bracken fronds at night', with words by Norman Nicholson, is included. **Paul Leddington Wright** (b.1951) made arrangements of 'O Come, O Come, Emmanuel' and 'We three kings' which have been included.[32]

A nice touch in the book is the inclusion of 'Wassail' by **Jonathan Willcocks** (b.1953), son of Sir David, who had been a chorister at King's and then, after studying at Clifton College, a choral scholar at Trinity College, Cambridge.

Philip Ledger (1937-2012) succeeded Willcocks at King's in 1974, remaining until 1982 when Stephen Cleobury took over. Born in Bexhill-on-Sea, he studied at King's, and became the youngest cathedral organist of his day when in 1961 he was appointed to Chelmsford Cathedral, and soon became a leading light in the foundation of the music department at East Anglia University. In 1968 he became director of the Aldeburgh Festival, established by Benjamin Britten and Peter Pears, and took up the post of Director of the Cambridge University Musical Society (CUMS) in 1973. In 1982 he moved to Glasgow to become Principal of the Royal Scottish Academy of Music and Drama. None of his work had appeared in *CFC1-4*, so it was fitting that 'The Bell Carol', with words by Longfellow, should be included in volume five. His arrangement of 'O Come, all ye faithful' with a new descant and final verse version also appears.

Stephen Cleobury (b.1948) has been Director of King's College Choir since 1982. He was organ scholar at St John's College under George Guest, before becoming sub-organist at Westminster Abbey and then, in 1979, Master of Music at Westminster (Roman Catholic) Cathedral. In 2009 he was awarded a CBE. In *CFC5* his

---

[32] See Idle, Christopher, "The Living Tradition".

arrangement of the German carol 'Blest Mary wanders through the thorn' is published.

John Scott (b.1956), a native of Wakefield, Yorkshire, became organ scholar at St John's College, Cambridge, between 1974 and 1978, studying under George Guest. From 1978-85 he managed to hold the post of assistant organist at both St Paul's and Southwark Cathedrals, crossing the river between services! In 1985 he focused entirely on St Paul's, where in 1990 he became Director of Music, a post he held until 2004 when he crossed the Atlantic to St Thomas' Church, Fifth Avenue, New York, NY. In 2004 he was awarded the LVO. His arrangement of Sullivan's 'It Came Upon the Midnight Clear' is included in CFC5.

A NOTE ON THE TEXTS OF *CAROLS FOR CHOIRS*

Sadly the texts used in the CFC volumes are incompatible with many hymn books and recent research. Nevertheless, perhaps inevitably, the *CFC* texts have become the ones sung at Christmas services and concerts. Some but not all were taken from *EH* (which is printed and distributed by OUP), but nowadays there is often a problem as competing texts are insupportable in a service or concert. Choirs are not keen to sing different texts from those included in the *CFC* choir books and so they survive, immune to scholarship, modern trends or inclusive language.

King's College Carols

Finally we turn to the fount and outpouring of all this carolling: the world famous 'Festival of Nine Lessons and Carols' and its offshoot 'Carols from Kings'. It is important to distinguish between the liturgical phenomenon that is the former, repeated worldwide for decades, and the latter service, recorded in advance and broadcast on Christmas Eve. 'Carols from Kings' has seven readings, some of which are not Biblical, whereas the older liturgy follows a set pattern of nine Bible readings, and the two have to some extent gone their separate ways. 'Carols from Kings' is unique in the world of Christmas music, indeed of hymnody: there is no festival like it, for popularity, significance or influence. It both feeds and consumes the Christmas carol market, commissioning new works and showcasing those in the *CFC* books. Through it the English carol-singing tradition is kept buoyant and world-class. The conglomeration of resources, talent and enthusiasm which successive directors of music have brought to their role at King's has ensured steady growth and an insurmountable position at the top of the Christmas tree. The King's Christmas is a quality product, marketed superbly.

THE NINE LESSONS AND CAROLS

The origins of the 'Service of Nine Lessons and Carols' are not to be found in Cambridge itself, although its inventor was educated at Trinity. **Edward Benson** (1829-96) was ordained deacon in 1852, the same year he took up a schoolmastership at Rugby School. He was Headmaster of Wellington School and became Chancellor of Lincoln Cathedral in 1872 before being appointed the first Bishop of Truro in 1877. He became Archbishop of Canterbury in 1883. It was while at Truro that he devised a liturgy for Christmas Eve which he called 'Nine Lessons with Carols – Festival Service for Christmas Eve' and it was first used in Truro Cathedral on Christmas Eve, 1880. The famous tradition is that Truro Cathedral was little more than a wooden structure at the time, and by scheduling it at 10pm he hoped to keep the men out of the pubs. This original 'Nine Lessons' tradition survives in many places and offers the traditional reading through of the story of redemption commencing with a child (or chorister) reading the story of Adam and Eve in the garden, culminating with a senior cleric reading the first Chapter of St John, with the congregation standing.

It was another 38 years before **Arthur Henry Mann** (1850-1929), who was organist of King's College from 1876 to 1929, took up the idea, guided by the Dean of Chapel, **Eric Milner White** (1884-1963). On Christmas Eve 1918, with the Great War recently ended, a new tradition was born. Ten years later the BBC began to broadcast it worldwide, and have done so every year, with the exception of 1930, yet throughout the Second World War. Between 1941 and 1945 the organist in charge was **Harold Darke** (1888-1976), who is most famous for his ethereal setting of Christina Rossetti's 'In the Bleak Midwinter'. Darke died in Cambridge on 28 November 1976, even though his musical career was, with the exception of his wartime tenure at King's, spent in London.

CAROLS FROM KINGS

The King's Christmas continued to evolve, and spawned 'Carols from King's', a recorded festival broadcast on television, firstly in 1954, and then again in 1964 and every year thereafter. What many people think is 'Nine Lessons and Carols' is not in fact, and the current King's approach is to have seven readings, and not all of them from the Bible. However, while 'Carols from King's' and 'The Festival of Nine Lessons' have diverged, they will always be inexorably linked, and as a joint phenomenon have held sway worldwide as the fount of many Christmastide blessings.

For many, Christmas is not Christmas without a traditional carol service, and the archetypal carol service is the 'Nine Lessons', the very conception of which includes the singing of both congregational and 'choir' carols. It is a participatory concert, with spiritual and religious foundations, grounded in the familiar. And if the 'Nine Lessons' is the archetypal carol service, then Cambridge has claimed and nurtured that tradition, and so will always be the Christmas Carol Capital of the World.

CAMBRIDGE HYMN-WRITERS FROM THE SIXTEENTH TO THE TWENTIETH CENTURIES

David M. Thompson

Congregational hymnody was not part of the worship of the medieval Church, except for the office hymns sung in religious houses. The Reformation, particularly in Germany, saw a great change in this respect. Nevertheless, although Cambridge was the theological birthplace of the English Reformation, not a large number of hymn-writers studied there. **Miles Coverdale** (1488-1569) deserves the first place for two reasons, his early publication of a translation of hymns and psalms from German in 1535, over a decade before Sternhold's metrical psalter; and because his translation of the psalms for the Great Bible of 1539 became that used in Cranmer's *Book of Common Prayer*, and therefore the first love in the Church of England. As an Augustinian friar from the late 1510's in the order's house in Cambridge, he influenced the prior, Robert Barnes, in favour of reform. He graduated around 1526-27, but was subsequently forced into exile by Wolsey, and found his way to Antwerp, where he worked with Tyndale in translating the Bible into English. Coverdale's own translation (using the work of other writers) was dedicated to the king, published in 1535, and was based on the Vulgate, not the original Hebrew and Greek.

On his return to England in the same year Coverdale published some forty *Goostly Psalmes and Spirituall Songs Drawen out of the Holy Scripture* in London: nearly half of these were based on Luther's Hymnal. With the patronage of Thomas Cromwell and in a mood more receptive to reform, his talents were drawn on for the Great Bible, for which he made various changes to his earlier translations as a result of knowledge of the German translations from the Hebrew and Greek. Forced into exile again in 1540 after the fall of Cromwell he did not return until after Henry VIII's death. He was Bishop of Exeter from 1551 to 1553, but did not resume his bishopric after Mary's death in 1558.

Although the use of hymns was not common before the later seventeenth century, several writers had their religious verse subsequently used as hymns. Among these the single best known is probably the version of 'Veni Creator Spiritus' by **John Cosin** (1595-1672), fellow of Gonville and Caius College, and later master of Peterhouse. He became Bishop of Durham in 1660 after the Restoration. The 'Veni Creator' is a ninth century hymn: Cosin's translation, first published in his *Collection of Private Devotions* (1627) has the distinction of being one of the two hymns authorized for use in the Church of England by its inclusion in Service for the Ordination of Priests in the BCP of 1662 (the other being the earlier Common Metre version).

George Herbert (1593-1633), undergraduate and fellow of Trinity College, and university Orator at Cambridge, had a varied career before his premature death from consumption in 1633. At first, as the careers of his two brothers suggested, he seemed to be moving in the direction of politics. He was briefly MP for Montgomery in 1624, but at that time he applied to the Archbishop of Canterbury for ordination as deacon. By 1626 he had been made a non-residentiary canon of Lincoln cathedral and prebendary of Leighton Bromswold in Huntingdonshire, where he rebuilt the ruined church. This was when he met Nicholas Ferrar at Little Gidding. From 1630 he served as rector of Bemerton, near Salisbury.

Herbert's religious poetry has been described as 'among the most moving and effective in the English language'. Those poems well known as hymns come from *The Temple*, a collection of his verse published after his death in 1633 (though begun much earlier), edited by Ferrar. In the seventeenth century the appeal of his poetry was very wide – from Charles I in prison, to one of Cromwell's chaplains, to Richard Baxter, who described it as combining 'Heart-work and Heaven-work'. The emphasis on Herbert's personal holiness (which is not in doubt) and his friendship with Ferrar probably led to his being regarded as more exclusively committed to the high church Anglican position than he was. His elder brother, Edward, Lord Herbert of Cherbury, made a reputation for himself as the first thoroughgoing rationalist in religion writing in English.

The metrical structure of Herbert's verse does not make for easy musical settings, and probably most of those that can easily be made into singable hymns have now been used. Interestingly more were included in *H&P* (though only three survived into *Singing the Faith* in 2011) from the Methodists and *R&S* from the United Reformed Church respectively than in *NEH*. The five best-known are 'King of glory, King of peace', 'Let all the world in every corner sing', 'Teach me, my God and King', 'The God of love my Shepherd is' and 'Come, my Way, my Truth, my Life' (which is more often sung as an anthem). Their use as hymns, particularly in their original form, dates from the early twentieth century, apart from 'Let all the world', which did appear in some late nineteenth century books.

John Milton (1608-74) was an undergraduate at Christ's College, matriculating in 1625. He never fulfilled his intention of taking his BD degree and being ordained, because in the 1640s he became embroiled in anti-episcopal polemics, and later defended the right of the people to bring a tyrant to judgement. His defence of toleration moved him from Presbyterian sympathies to a position more closely aligned with the Independents, though he was never recorded as a member of a Congregational church. The hymns for which he is remembered are all psalm paraphrases, of which he wrote nineteen in all. The earliest and best known is 'Let us with a gladsome mind' (Psalm 136), written when he was a fifteen year-old pupil at St Paul's school in London, and published in his *Poems* of 1645. The other still in regular use is 'The Lord will come and not be slow', possibly inspired by the Scottish metrical psalter and based on a translation from the Hebrew (though using the cadences of the Authorized Version) of Psalms 82, 85 and 86. In its reduced modern form it is principally concerned with justice and peace; but the complete original also contained a strong critique of a corrupt and badly governed society, which gave it an obviously contemporary resonance. Although completed in 1648, this group of nine psalms was not published until the second edition of Milton's *Poems* in English and Latin of 1673. The other hymn, found in some older books (and also *The Cambridge Hymnal*), is a rendering of Psalm 84 from the 1648 group: 'How lovely are thy dwellings fair'.

John Mason (1646-94) was one of the first ministers in the Church of England actively to encourage the singing of hymns. The son of a dissenting minister and father of another, he went up to Clare College in 1661, graduating in 1665 and receiving his MA in 1668. Following ordination he was vicar of Stantonbury, Buckinghamshire and then rector of Water Stratford in the same county, where he remained until his death. In 1683 he published *Spiritual Songs, or Songs of Praise*, which subsequently went through sixteen editions, the last of which came out in 1761. He was a friend of Richard Baxter, who called him 'the glory of the Church of England.' The hymn for which he is best known today is 'How shall I sing that majesty', which has been given a fresh lease of life by the tune written by Kenneth Naylor, formerly Head of Music at the Leys School, Cambridge – COE FEN. In his final years Mason was best known for his millenarianism, and shortly before his death in 1694 he claimed to have had a vision of Christ; a group of followers continued that tradition into the 1730's.

In addition a number of seventeenth century poets (Richard Crashaw, Phineas Fletcher, Robert Herrick, Thomas Campion, Edmund Spencer, Francis Quarles, Philip Howard, Henry More and John Dryden) wrote religious verse that has been used as hymns. Only occasionally are these still to be found in hymn books.

From the eighteenth century, **John Byrom** (1692-1763) was a student and fellow at Trinity College, who subsequently studied medicine in France and became a doctor, before succeeding to the family estates. His poem, 'Christians, awake, salute the happy morn', was written for his daughter as a Christmas present in 1749. Byrom's friend, John Wainwright, wrote the tune with which it remains associated the following year, and had it sung outside Byrom's house in Manchester. It was subsequently included in his posthumous *Poems*[33] of 1773, but was made popular when James Montgomery adapted it for the eighth edition of Thomas Cotterill's *Psalms and Hymns for Public and Private Use* (1819). Its popularity in the north of England only spread south with the publication of *Hymns Ancient and Modern* in 1861.

---

[33] The full title was *Miscellaneous Poems by John Byrom: Inventor of the Universal English Shorthand*

Rowland Hill (1744-1833) was one of the earliest Cambridge evangelicals. Educated at Shrewsbury and Eton, he was converted to an evangelical position by his elder brother, Richard, before coming to St John's College, Cambridge, as a pensioner. With ten or twelve friends he formed a religious society, which engaged in Bible study, visited the sick and those in prison and preached in Cambridge and its surrounding villages. After taking his BA in 1769, Hill spent four years in itinerant preaching. Heavily influenced by George Whitefield and John Berridge, he adopted a Calvinist position like many early Anglican evangelicals, which separated him from Wesleyan Methodism. He took his MA in 1772 and a year later persuaded the Bishop of Bath and Wells to ordain him deacon as curate at Kingston, near Taunton. In 1773 he married and settled at Wotton under Edge, Gloucestershire, where he built a chapel. He did not immediately give up his curacy, but spent twelve years preaching in Wiltshire, Gloucestershire, Somerset and London, where he built the Surrey Chapel in 1783 and ministered there for nearly fifty years. Like John Wesley, he combined Anglican orders with effective nonconformist ministry: he was one of the founders of the London Missionary Society and on the first Committee of the Religious Tract Society. He published *A Collection of Hymns and Psalms for the use of the Poor* in 1774 and *A Collection of Psalms and Hymns, chiefly intended for Public Worship* in 1783, which was revised and expanded several times before his death, and *A Collection of Hymns for Children* (1808). None of his hymns is in common use today.

Christopher Smart (1722-71) entered Pembroke College, Cambridge in 1739, where he became an accomplished classical scholar, winning the Craven university scholarship in 1742. He received his BA in 1744 and became a fellow of Pembroke in the following year. A riotous episode in London in 1747 nearly cost him his fellowship. However, in 1749 he left Cambridge for good. His most original works were written while he was in St Luke's Hospital (the 'Madhouse') between 1757 and 1763. Smart does not fit into any stereotype, though he has been seen as a precursor of William Blake. John Julian did not include him in his *Dictionary of*

Hymnology, [34] probably because Smart's *Hymns and Spiritual Songs for the Feasts and Festivals of the Church of England,* published with his *Translation of the Psalms of David* in 1765, had been entirely unnoticed at the time. It was the discovery and publication of the manuscript of 'Jubilate Agno' ('Rejoice in the Lamb') in 1939 and Benjamin Britten's setting of it in his cantata of the same name in 1944 that refocused attention on Smart's religious verse. Only some of it was written to be sung; but *The Cambridge Hymnal* included three hymns, and *NEH, R&S,* and *Common Praise* included the Christmas verses, 'Where is this stupendous stranger', rescued for the American Episcopal *Hymnal 1940* [35] by Francis Bland Tucker.

Because nonconformists were excluded from Cambridge between 1662 and 1856, there are no representatives from the University. However, **Robert Robinson** (1735-99) was one of the great eighteenth-century ministers in the town. Having been impressed by a sermon by George Whitefield on 'The Wrath to Come', he struggled to find assurance for three years. In 1755 he began to preach, and after ministries at a Calvinistic Methodist chapel in Mildenhall, Suffolk, and an Independent congregation in Norwich, he was minister at the Stone Yard Baptist Church (now St Andrew's Street) from 1761 to 1790. Here he impressed members of the University as well as his own congregation. He wrote a number of hymns, of which the best known are 'Come, Thou fount of every blessing' and 'Mighty God, while angels bless Thee'.

Sir **Robert Grant** (1785-1838) was another evangelical. The son of Charles Grant, Chairman of the East India Company, he was privately educated by the evangelical minister, Henry Venn, before entering Magdalene College, Cambridge, in 1795. He graduated as Third Wrangler and second Chancellor's Medallist in 1801, and became a fellow of Magdalene in 1802, receiving his MA in 1804. After being called to the Bar in 1807, he became an MP in 1818, and remained so until family lobbying brought him the Governorship of Bombay in 1834. He died unexpectedly in 1838. Most of his

---

[34] Julian, J. A. *Dictionary of Hymnology,* John Murray, London, 1892; Revised Edition with New Supplement, 1907

[35] *The Hymnal of the Protestant Episcopal Church in the United States of America,* Church Publishing, Inc., New York, NY, 1940

hymns were contributed to the *Christian Observer* between 1806 and 1815. The best known still in use is 'O worship the King', based on Psalm 104, first published in Edward Bickersteth's *Christian Psalmody* (1833), and corrected in the posthumous edition of twelve of his hymns by his brother (1839).

There were three nineteenth-century hymn writers from the high church tradition: Christopher Wordsworth, John Ellerton and John Mason Neale. By comparison with the other two, **Christopher Wordsworth** (1807-85) seems almost minor. He was William Wordsworth's nephew – his father was William's youngest brother, Master of Trinity College, Cambridge (1820-46) and a traditional high churchman. He distinguished himself at Winchester, entering Trinity College in 1826, graduating as senior classic in the Classical Tripos in 1830 and winning the first Chancellor's medal for classical studies. He was immediately elected to a fellowship at Trinity. Ordained priest in 1835, he became Public Orator of the University in the following year and also Headmaster of Harrow, before receiving a canonry of Westminster in 1844. He became Bishop of Lincoln in 1868. His hymns are found in his collection, *The Holy Year* [36](1862). *NEH* has seven, and other hymnbooks fewer. The best known are probably 'Gracious Spirit, Holy Ghost', 'Songs of thankfulness and praise' and 'See the conqueror mounts in triumph'. Christopher Wordsworth was also more inclined to the Eastern Church and later the Old Catholics, than the Roman Church.

John Ellerton (1826-93) entered Trinity College in 1845, graduating in 1849, and was ordained in 1850. He was a life-long friend of Henry Bradshaw, later Cambridge University librarian, and Fenton Anthony Hort, the New Testament scholar. Like many in his circle as an undergraduate, he was influenced by F.D. Maurice, and spent his early years studying the writings of the Christian Socialists, particularly Charles Kingsley. Although he wrote over eighty hymns and several translations from Latin, his main influence on hymnody was through editing and compiling hymnbooks. He edited *Hymns for Schools and Bible Classes* (1859), and, with

---

[36] Wordsworth, Christopher, *The Holy Year: Or, Hymns for Sundays and Holydays, and for Other Occasions*, Rivingtons, London, 1862

Bishop Walsham How and others, *Church Hymns* (1871); he also published *Notes and Illustrations of Church Hymns* (1881), which was one of the earliest hymn book Companions. He was a consultant for the third edition of *Hymns Ancient and Modern* in 1889, and published a definitive edition of his own hymns in *Hymns Original and Translated* (1888). Almost certainly his best-loved hymn is 'The day thou gavest, Lord, is ended', written for *A Liturgy for Missionary Meetings* (1870) and then published in *Church Hymns*. Queen Victoria chose it to be sung at her Diamond Jubilee. *Common Praise* contains five and *NEH* seven of his hymns.

John Mason Neale (1818-66) was the greatest hymnologist that Cambridge has produced, and many of his hymns and translations are still in regular use today. Neale won a scholarship to Trinity College, Cambridge, in 1836 and, although he was probably the best classicist of the year, he failed mathematics and therefore secured only a pass degree in 1840. He was ordained deacon in 1841 and priest in 1842, accepting the living of Crawley in Sussex. However, he was dogged by ill-health, particularly consumption, and spent his early years commuting between Sussex and Madeira. Like John Henry Newman, Neale had moved from evangelicalism to anglo-catholicism, but unlike the Oxford men he was never attracted by Rome, particularly its understanding of papal supremacy. In the critical period of the early 1840's he tried to steady the Anglican boat through the Tractarian waves, and to demonstrate that the Church of England had an orthodox catholic heritage.

In large part that explains his interest in Eastern Orthodoxy, and while in Madeira in these years he began to write his *A History of the Holy Eastern Church*. The Ecclesiological Society, which he and Benjamin Webb had founded in Cambridge at the end of the 1830's, reflected their desire for the 'correct' restoration of churches, that is, to a pattern based essentially on gothic architecture, particularly the Decorated style of the fourteenth century. All Saints', Margaret Street, London (designed by William Butterfield, built 1850-59) was their ideal church. Neale and Webb emphasized the symbolism of each part of the church building, and supported the re-introduction of vestments and incense (in which the Oxford men had relatively little interest). He was offered the

Wardenship of Sackville College, East Grinstead in 1846, a college for a small group of pensioners, where he spent the rest of his life. His restoration of the chapel and reform of its services attracted the unfavourable attention of his bishop and his licence to celebrate in the diocese was suspended for twelve years. Undaunted, in 1854 he began a Sisterhood in co-operation with the rector's daughter, which also proved controversial.

The limitation of his clerical duties left him free to research and to write, and he exploited this opportunity to the full. As well as the various volumes of his *History of the Eastern Church*, he also translated *The Primitive Liturgies of S. Mark, S Clement, S. James, S. Chrysostom and S. Basil*. His own original compositions were contained in *Hymns for Children* (1842) in three series, *Hymns for the Sick* (1843), *Hymns for the Young* (1844), *Carols for Christmas and Eastertide* (1853) and *Songs and Ballads for the People* (1855); his translations were in *Medieval Hymns and Sequences* (1851), The Hymnal Noted (1852), Hymns of the Eastern Church (1862), *Hymns, Chiefly Medieval, on the Joys and Glories of Paradise* (1865) and *Original Sequences, Hymns, and other Ecclesiastical Verses* (1866). Most of those by Neale which have retained their popularity are translations, a large number coming from the *Medieval Hymns and Sequences*, such as 'All glory, laud and honour', 'Blessed city, heavenly Salem', 'O come, O come, Emmanuel', 'To the name of our salvation', 'O sons and daughters, let us sing'. 'Good Christians all, rejoice' and 'A great and mighty wonder' come from *Carols for Christmastide*, whilst 'Come, ye faithful, raise the strain' and 'The day of resurrection' come from *Hymns of the Eastern Church*. NEH contains thirty-two Neale hymns and translations, including several of the Office Hymns. Some of his own are 'Around the throne of God' (*Hymns for Children*) and 'O happy band of pilgrims', which, though it appeared in *Hymns of the Eastern Church*, was substantially Neale's own composition. Simply to list these is adequate testament to Neale's significance, and the range of his material.

George Wallace Briggs (1875-1959) was the most significant Cambridge hymn writer in the first half of the twentieth century[37], and may still be rather under-estimated. He was one of the founders of The Hymn Society of Great Britain and Ireland, and Chairman of its Executive Committee for many years. Because he came just before the 'hymn revolution' of the second half of the century, and was still using 'thee' and thou' (which went rapidly out of fashion after 1960), some of his hymns are neglected today. Briggs was a scholar of Emmanuel College (1894-97), where he obtained first-class honours in Classics. After seven years' service as a Royal Navy chaplain, he became vicar of St Andrew's, Norwich in 1909 and rector of Loughborough in 1918. He was a canon of Leicester (1927-34) and then a canon of Worcester until his retirement. The Leicestershire County Council published *Prayers and Hymns for use in Schools*[38] in 1927, for which Briggs was mainly responsible. He was involved in the production of *The Daily Service*,[39] which was adopted by many Education Authorities. Behind these books was the strong influence of *Songs of Praise*[40] (1925), edited by Percy Dearmer, Ralph Vaughan Williams and Martin Shaw. Dearmer and Vaughan Williams had worked together on *EH* (1906), representing the high church tradition. *Songs of Praise* included much of that material, but also hymnody reflecting Dearmer's involvement in the Christian Socialist movement and the wider attempt in the aftermath of the First World War to create a hymnody more accessible to ordinary people. Briggs was one of those involved in the production of *Songs of Praise: Enlarged Edition* (1931), the influence of which was enormous, and because its material was used so widely in school assemblies it shaped the knowledge of hymns for at least a generation, beyond the churches as well as within them.

---

[37] Cambridge's contribution to the second half of the century, particularly through the *doyen* of modern hymn-writers, Bishop Timothy Dudley-Smith, is dealt with in Idle, Christopher, "The Living Tradition".

[38] *County of Leicester. Prayers & Hymns for use in Schools. The Hymn-book being an abridged edition of "Songs of Praise" together with a few additional hymns*, Oxford University Press, Oxford, 1927

[39] Briggs, G.W., Dearmer, Percy, Vaughan Williams, Ralph, Shaw, Martin (Eds.). *The Daily Service. Prayers and Hymns for Schools*, Oxford University Press, Oxford, 1939 (first edition; also various subsequent editions)

[40] Oxford University Press, Oxford, 1925; revised and enlarged edition, 1931

Songs of Praise evoked strong feelings. In their little skit, *Babylon Bruis'd and Mount Moriah Mended* (1940), two Fellows of Jesus College, Freddie Brittain and Bernard Manning, imagined a Visitation of Cambridge churches and college chapels like that of William Dowsing in 1643, to remove superstitious objects from parish churches. One of their chief targets was 'a Booke of rhymes and ditties entituled *Songes of Prayse*', copies of which they removed from several churches and chapels, along with *The Oxford Psalter*. **Bernard Lord Manning** (1892-1941) rescued the significance of nonconformist hymnody, particularly in his *The Hymns of Wesley and Watts* (1942), a posthumous collection of talks given to student societies in Cambridge in the 1930s. Manning was a medieval historian, with a strong sense of the Calvinist tradition in his own Congregationalism. He was scathing in his dismissal of anyone without a sense of history and indeed continuity in the Christian tradition. Thus he dismisses 'the rascals who compiled [the Wesleyan Hymn Book] of 1904' as robbing Methodists of their heritage, i.e. by finally breaking away from the pattern of Wesley's *Hymns for the Use of the People called Methodists*. While praising Charles Wesley for his combination of dogma, experience and mysticism 'in verse so simple that it could be understood ... by plain men', Manning also noted that the great difference between Isaac Watts and Wesley was that Watts saw the Cross as 'planted on a globe hung in space, surrounded by the vast distances of the universe'. Manning packed into a little book of barely a hundred and fifty pages more insights that many to be found in much longer works.

Briggs published two collections of his own work, *Songs of Faith* (1945) and *Hymns of the Faith* (1957).[41] Although the number of his hymns included in recent collections has been declining (*H&P*: six; *NEH*: three; *R&S*: eight; *Common Praise*: five; *Singing the Faith*: one), some have remained favourites: 'Come, risen Lord, and be our guest' at Holy Communion; 'Christ is the world's true light'; and 'Now is eternal life' for baptism. 'Son of the Lord most high', while retaining strong 'Christ the worker' influences, is also a useful hymn in the period after Epiphany for the 'hidden years' between the nativity and baptism of Jesus. Briggs also began to

---

[41] Both Oxford University Press, Oxford

tackle the changes in the way in which the Word of God in Scripture is understood, for example in 'Light of the world, from all truth proceeding', 'The Spirit of the Lord revealed' or 'God has spoken', which was one of his late hymns in 1953.

Briggs co-operated with **Eric Milner-White** (1884-1963), who was Dean of King's College (1918-41) in the production of *Daily Prayer* (1941), which is a reminder that Cambridge has been significant for the way its colleges have contributed to and developed the liturgical tradition of the country since J.M. Neale. Milner-White introduced the annual Christmas Eve Service of Nine Lessons and Carols at King's (originally based on a pattern introduced by another Cambridge man, Bishop Benson, at Truro Cathedral in 1881); this has attained world-wide significance through the BBC's decision to broadcast it in 1928. The era of records and CD's has made the choirs of St John's, Trinity and Clare Colleges world-famous as well. The Cambridge musical tradition had been revived in the late nineteenth century by Sir Charles Villiers Stanford, Professor of Music from 1887 to 1924. In the twentieth century a series of Directors of Music strengthened this, both through college chapel choirs and wider student activities, drawing on the unrivalled musical talent among the university's junior members.

Finally, reference should be made to *The Cambridge Hymnal* (1967), edited by David Holbrook and Elizabeth Poston, which was an 'experiment' (in the editors' words) to see whether it was possible to compile a collection of hymns for children to avoid those requiring 'attention to meaning' to be suspended, which 'no intelligent adult could sing … if he really considered what he was saying'. From a collection of ten thousand hymns the editors selected just over a hundred. It was 'an undenominational collection' (by contrast with the inter-denominational appeal of *Songs of Praise*). Whether it changed the face of hymn singing in schools is doubtful; but it was published just at the point where hymns were either disappearing or being replaced by more anodyne worship songs. Whatever view is taken, it is an interesting commentary on the 'Cambridge tradition'.

CAMBRIDGE TUNES AND SOME MUSICIANS PAST

Valerie Ruddle

Hymn Tunes named CAMBRIDGE

A great number of musicians have studied at Cambridge University and, over the centuries, some have made significant marks on the life of the city. Several hymn tunes have been named CAMBRIDGE, each with a different metre.

The earliest is by **John Randall** (1715-99) who, after graduating at Cambridge, was appointed organist at King's College in 1745 and remained so until his death fifty-four years later. From 1755 until 1799 he was also Professor of Music. His Common Metre tune was called CAMBRIDGE NEW, so there may have been an earlier one. In 1794 he published *A Collection of Psalm and Hymn Tunes*[42] in which the tune UNIVERSITY appeared anonymously. This had previously appeared, attributed to **Charles Collignon** (1725-85) in *A Collection of Psalms and Hymns the use of Parish Churches*[43] edited by Pieter Hellendaal. No other composition by Collignon is known. He was Professor of Anatomy at Cambridge University from 1753 until 1785 and was described by a colleague as 'a perfect skeleton himself, absolutely a walking shadow, nothing but skin and bone.'

The Short Metre tune CAMBRIDGE often set to Charles Wesley's 'A charge to keep have I' is by **Ralph Harrison** (1748-1810), who has no evident connection with the city. Born in Derbyshire in 1748, the son of a Dissenting Protestant Minister, Harrison was educated at Warrington Academy, the cradle of Unitarianism in the eighteenth century, and spent most of his life in Manchester as a Unitarian Minister. His tune, unnamed at the time, appeared in his *Sacred Harmony, A Collection of Psalm Tunes Ancient and Modern*

---

[42] The full title is *A Collection of Psalm and Hymn Tunes, some of which are new and others by permission of the authors, with six Chants and Te Deums, calculated for the use of congregations in general*

[43] Cambridge, 1793

(1784).[44] Harrison appears to have had no formal musical training, but he went to great lengths to explain that the first part of his *Collection* contained 'the more easy tunes', such as were suitable for congregations, while the second part had 'tunes of greater diversity of style, more fit for practitioners of choirs of singers'. He had 'purposely avoided those more light and flimsy airs which abase the subject to which they belong.'[45] S.S. Wesley harmonised Harrison's melody for his *European Psalmist*,[46] and called it CAMBERWELL (not to be confused with Michael Brierley's tune of that name). It was first named CAMBRIDGE in *Wesley's Hymns* (1877)[47] for no obvious reason.

The popularity of the tune CAMBRIDGE by **Charles Wood** (1866-1926) has been hampered by the text for which it was written. 'Christ who knows all his sheep' by Richard Baxter (1615-91) is usually found in the 'Death and Judgement' section of a hymn book, not frequently visited, and the irregular metre of Wood's very singable tune prevents it from being used for other texts. Born in Armagh, Ireland, in 1866, Wood was one of the first students at the Royal College of Music, London, studying composition with Stanford and Parry as well as horn and piano. His studies continued at Selwyn College, Cambridge, and then at Gonville and Caius College where he later became its first Director of Music and Organist. He was regarded as a distinguished teacher, with Ralph Vaughan Williams and Herbert Howells among his pupils. He succeeded Stanford as University Professor of Music in 1924 and

---

[44] The full title is *Sacred harmony, A collection of Psalm tunes, ancient and modern : containing a great variety of the most approved plain & simple airs, with a considerable number of tunes in verse & chorus & fugues, the whole set in four parts and arranged under their several metres & keys, with a figured bass for the pianoforte & organ, together with a selection of canons, chants, & c. & an introduction to the art of singing.*
[45] Lightwood, James, *The Music of the Methodist Hymn Book*, Epworth Press, London, 1935
[46] Wesley, Samuel Sebastian, *The European Psalmist*, Novello & Company, London & New York, 1872
[47] Wesley, John, *Wesley's Hymns and New Supplement with Tunes. A Collection of Hymns for the Use of the People Called Methodists – by the Rev. John Wesley, M.A. – with a New Supplement. Edition with Tunes.* Wesleyan Conference Office, London, 1877

died two years later. He greatly influenced the development of musical life in Cambridge.

CAMBRIDGE, by **Charles Fishwick** (1878-1963), was written for Mary Hearn's 8886 text, 'Just as I am, thine own to be' and was published in *Redemption Hymnal*,[48] *The Keswick Hymn Book*[49] and several similar publications, but has not become well-known.

The most recently composed tune known to bear the city's name was written by New Zealander **Colin Gibson** (b.1933). Taking a sabbatical year from teaching English Literature at the University of Otago, Dunedin, NZ, he was enjoying the privilege of a fellowship at Clare College, Cambridge, in 1992 when he received the words of 'Christ of the sad face' from the author and fellow New Zealander Shirley Erena Murray. Colin, a writer, editor and lay preacher as well as a musician, says that the tune was composed at a battered old piano in a rented house in Trumpington, on the outskirts of Cambridge. He has led many workshops on hymnody and church music and has taken part in some of our Hymn Society Conferences.

Trinity College

Founded by King Henry VIII in 1546, Trinity is the largest college of Cambridge University today and consists of a Master, a hundred and sixty Fellows, mostly engaged in teaching, about three hundred postgraduates and about six hundred undergraduates. Visitors have access to some of the grounds and the chapel for a modest £1. Many famous people have studied at Trinity, including the mathematician Isaac Newton (1643-1727), the scientist Francis Bacon (1561-1626) and the poet Alfred Lord Tennyson (1809-92) whose statues grace the ante-chapel. Memorials to other former students cover the south and north walls. These include the musicians Charles Villiers Stanford, Alan Gray, Ralph Vaughan Williams and **Thomas Walmisley**, whose inscription is the only one not in Latin. Under a few bars of his setting of Psalm 124, it reads:

---

[48] *Redemption Hymnal*, Rickfords Hill Publishing Ltd, Wendover, 1951
[49] Keswick Convention, *The Keswick Hymn Book*, Marshall, Morgan & Scott, London, various editions at different dates

In memory of
Thomas Attwood Walmisley M.A. Mus. Doc.
Organist of the College 1833 – 1856
Professor of Music in the University 1836-1856
Born Jan 21 1814   Died Jan 17 1856

Thomas Walmisley was organist, not only of Trinity College but also of St. John's College as well as deputising at King's College and the University Church, resulting in occasionally playing for eight services on a Sunday!

Charles Villiers Stanford (1852-1924) was born in Dublin and showed great musical ability at an early age. Like many musicians who gained entry to Cambridge colleges through organ or choral scholarship, Stanford entered Queen's College, Cambridge as a choral scholar but read classics to satisfy his father's wishes. However nothing could keep him away from music for long. He helped to found the Cambridge Musical Society in 1872 and became its conductor while still a student. He was organist of Trinity College from 1873 until 1892 and Professor of Music from 1887 until his death. When the Royal College of Music was opened in London, he became its first Professor of Composition and Orchestral Playing while retaining his positions in Cambridge.

Alan Gray (1855-1935) studied law but then devoted himself entirely to music. After ten years as Director of Music at Wellington College, he succeeded Stanford to the Trinity Chapel organ stool in 1893. He was conductor of the Cambridge University Musical Society and composed a wide variety of music. His hymn tunes BATTLE CRY and HOSANNA, published in *Hymns Ancient and Modern Revised* (1950) and *The Baptist Hymn Book* respectively, have not been retained in subsequent books.

Ralph Vaughan Williams (1872-1958) was born in the Gloucester village of Down Ampney, the name given to his most well-known hymn tune. After reading history and music at Trinity College, he became one of Britain's most significant composers. His most important contribution to hymnody was through folksong. He was an early member of the English Folk Song Society, founded in 1899, and on a three-day visit to Norfolk in 1905, collected over forty songs in public houses, from field workers and by the quayside. The melody of 'Young Henry, the poacher' became KING'S LYNN, the tune for G.K. Chesterton's 'O God of earth and altar' and appeared with many other similar adaptations in *EH* of which Vaughan Williams was Musical Editor. Of his original tunes SINE NOMINE ('For all the saints who from their labours rest') and DOWN AMPNEY ('Come down, O Love Divine') are sung widely today.

The Leys School

A significant part in the life of Cambridge has been played by The Leys School, an Independent School established in 1875 as a Methodist School for Boys, and now co-educational, day and boarding, for over five hundred students aged from eleven to eighteen. Its music masters have included Arthur Henry Mann, Edward Woodall Naylor and Kenneth Nicholson Naylor, all of whom have tunes in today's hymn books.

Arthur Henry Mann (1850-1929) vowed that he would never sing again once his time as a chorister at Norwich Cathedral ended, but he went on to become a successful church organist and highly acclaimed choir trainer, serving The Leys School as Organist and Director of Music, 1897-1929. The school chapel was opened in 1902 and, as its first organist, Mann made the accompaniments to chapel services something to remember. A colourful memorial inscription under a mosaic of Judas Maccabaeus is on the organ. His hymn tune LASUS, written for 'Come, gracious Spirit, heavenly dove' for Tettenhall Parish Church, Derbyshire, where he was organist before coming to Cambridge, is still sung today. WORSHIP for 'Wise men, seeking Jesus' and ANGEL'S SONG for 'I love to hear the story', have gone out of fashion. However Mann's main contribution to the musical life of Cambridge was as organist at King's College for fifty-three years (1874-1929) and University organist for thirty-two years (1897-1929). Organ scholarships at King's College have been funded from an A.H. Mann legacy since 1931. So far thirty-two young organists have benefitted, including David Willcocks (from 1939 to 1947).

Edward Woodall Naylor (1867-1934) was a chorister at York Minster, where his father was organist, 1883-97, and his association with Cambridge began when he became a choral scholar at Emmanuel College, Cambridge in 1884. After further studies at the Royal College of Music and holding various organ posts in London, Edward returned to Cambridge in 1897 as organist of Emmanuel College and assistant music master at The Leys School. From 1902 he was also College Lecturer in Music for over thirty years and University lecturer in Music History, 1926-1932. His Saturday morning lectures were so popular that the same lecture was sometimes repeated. He was considered an outstanding teacher, performer and author, his most important literary work being *Shakespeare and Music*,[50] which has influenced the choice of music for many Shakespeare productions. Naylor's FROM STRENGTH TO STRENGTH ('Soldiers of Christ, Arise') first appeared on a leaflet for Emmanuel College Chapel in 1902, was first published in *The Public School Hymn Book*[51] and has become increasingly popular.

Charles Naylor (1869-1945), Edward's brother, who also graduated from Emmanuel College, has contributed far more to hymnody than Edward. He was Music Adviser to the editorial committee of the Methodist School Hymnal (1911) in which forty-

---

[50] First published London & New York, 1896; revised edition, Da Capo Press and Benjamin Blom, New York, 1931

[51] *The Public School Hymn Book*, Novello & Company, London, 1919, revised 1949

one of his tunes can be found, including DERWENT ('Jesus, friend of little children'). He had a successful career in Harrogate, Yorkshire, as an organist, teacher and conductor.

Kenneth Nicholson Naylor (1931-97), no relation to the above, read music at Madgalene College, Cambridge, before becoming music master and then Director of Music (1953-80) at The Leys School. He had a special gift of being able to make schoolboys enjoy singing and wrote a handful of hymn tunes that would appeal to them, including COE FEN, written for 'How shall I sing that majesty' and now regarded as one of the best tunes of the twentieth century. Lionel Dakers, writing in *Beauty Beyond Words*,[52] refers to the tune as one that 'does everything a hymn tune ideally should do in terms of melody and harmony, with an unerring sense of climax where needed.' It was named after a Nature Reserve adjacent to The Leys School and was first published with the words in *Praise and Thanksgiving* (1985).[53] Work is in progress to gather together all Kenneth Naylor's hymn tunes and other compositions.

Cambridge Discovery

The contribution to hymnody by George Frederick Handel (1685-1759) is far greater than is often realised, although most of the Handelian tunes we sing were adapted from his oratorios after his death. His friends included John Rich, proprietor of Covent Garden Theatre, where many of his operas were performed, and his wife, who was one of the first members of the Methodist Society. It seems likely that she showed Handel a copy of *Twenty-four Hymns on the Great Festivals* (1746) by Charles Wesley. Each hymn had a florid tune by F.J. Lampe, a composer of theatre music. Handel apparently decided to write new tunes to three of the texts.

Seventy years later these were discovered by Charles Wesley's son, Samuel, a highly respected musician of the time (and father of the more famous Samuel Sebastian), who had permission to transcribe and publish musical manuscripts from the Fitzwilliam Library, Cambridge. On 13th September 1826 he wrote to his wife

---

[52] Dakers, Lionel, *Beauty Beyond Words: Enriching Worship Through Music*, Canterbury Press, Norwich, 2000
[53] Govver, R. (ed.), The Gresham Press, Henley-on-Thames, 1985

from the Castle Inn, Cambridge, 'All goes on well here. I have already copied six famous fine tunes from Handel's own manuscript, and what is uncommonly fortunate, they are all set to my Father's own words, so that my dear Father's Poetry must have highly delighted Handel. This circumstance will much forward the Work.'

There were actually only three tunes, all crammed onto one page of manuscript, and probably written between 1749 and 1752, before Handel began to go blind. The melody was in the soprano clef (middle C on the lowest line) with a figured bass, with the words of verse one interlined. A title was squeezed above the beginning of each tune which ended with four additional bars of figured bass, for the player to improvise a short postlude. The tunes are:

- **THE INVITATION – 'Sinnners , obey the Gospel word'**: This was called CANONS, the home of the Duke of Chandos, for whom Handel worked for some time. It is now sometimes called DEVONSHIRE or KENT.

- **DESIRING TO LOVE – 'O Love Divine, how sweet thou art'**: This was published as FITZWILLIAM, the library named after Richard, Viscount FitzWilliam, where the tunes were found.

- **ON THE RESURRECTION – 'Rejoice, the Lord is King'**: This was first called GOPSAL in W.H. Havergal's *Old Church Psalmody*, [54] after Gopsal Hall, near Ashby-de-la-Zouch, Leicestershire, the residence of Charles Jennens, who prepared the libretto for Handel's oratorio 'The Messiah', and with whom Handel often stayed. Gopsal Hall was demolished after army use, or rather, mis-use, during World War II.

Samuel Wesley published his findings immediately and, as he was especially keen that Methodists should sing the songs, he wrote to the Editor of the *Wesleyan-Methodist Magazine* in November 1826, 'I take the liberty of addressing you upon a subject which appears likely to prove both of interest and utility, especially to the Wesleyan Connexion. Having been honoured by the University of Cambridge with a Grace, authorising me to transcribe and publish any portions

---

[54] 2nd Edition, 1850

of the very valuable musical manuscripts in the Library of the Fitzwilliam Museum, of which privilege I have lately assiduously availed myself, I was very agreeably surprised at meeting with three Hymn Tunes, (most noble Melodies,) composed by our great Handel, (in his own hand-writing,) and set to words of my good Father.' Then, after explaining the metres in great detail, he suggested congregations would also find them useful for other texts, it being common practice for a few tunes to be used repeatedly. After publishing the three tunes in unison with accompaniment 'and very respectfully' presenting them to the 'Wesleyan Society at Large', Samuel Wesley issued an arrangement in open score 'for the convenience of choirs'.

Ely

In 970 a new Benedictine monastery for bachelor monks was built on a modest hill surrounded by flat fenland. Those who could not accept the austere life of celibacy were, according to a local legend, turned into eels – and so Ely got its name! A gleave, an implement for catching eels, can be seen in Ely Museum. The Isle of Ely disappeared after the Fens were drained in the eighteenth century.

Ely Cathedral was begun in 1083. When, in 1322, the original central tower collapsed, Alan of Walsingham, a leading Ely Monk, created the present octagonal Lantern Tower of wood, lead and glass. Each of the corner posts of the sixty-two feet high upper tower is cut from a single tree and weighs ten tons. It was an incredible feat of engineering!

The tune ELY was written by **Thomas Turton** (1780-1864) who was Bishop of Ely from 1845 until 1864. A Yorkshireman by birth, he graduated from St. Catharine's College in 1805 and was ordained in 1813, and returned to Cambridge as Regius Professor of Divinity in 1827. Turton was well versed in fine arts and had considerable musical skills. In his *A Collection of Psalm and Hymn*

Tunes (1844) [55] the tune now call ELY was named ST. CATHARINE.

Like many cathedrals today, the altar and choir stalls have been re-sited in front of the organ screen. Each choir kneeler commemorates, with a few bars of appropriate music, one of the thirty-two organists who have served there since 1443. One of the earliest is **Christopher Tye** (c.1505-c.1572), organist from 1541 for twenty years, and whose music is still sung today.

Another Ely organist is **Basil Harwood** (1859-1949) who was appointed in 1887 and resigned five years later, on the death of his father, to take over the running of the family estate near Bristol. His organ music and liturgical settings are occasionally heard today but his hymn tunes THORNBURY and LUCKINGTON are still widely sung.

Arthur Wills (b.1926) was organist from 1958 for thirty-two years. He combined his duties at Ely with those of a Professorship at the Royal Academy of Music, London, and he toured the world as a recitalist. He composed prolifically for the organ, including 'Variations on AMAZING GRACE' and the Symphonic Suite 'The Fenlands' for Brass Band and Organ.

The present Organist and Choir Director is **Paul Trepte** (b.1954), who succeeded Wills in 1990. He has gained a wide reputation not only as a recitalist but also as a conductor, adjudicator and examiner. Visitors may be lucky enough to hear him giving a lesson on the four-manual Harrison and Harrison organ, rebuilt in 1975. Visitors should also not miss a fascinating 1845 memorial to two young railway workers which includes a twenty-four lined poem entitled 'The Spiritual Railway', just outside the south door.

---

[55] The full title of the book is *A Collection of Psalm and Hymn Tunes, the best compositions in general use, many by eminent English and foreign musicians, which are now, for the first time, published in this country.*

PURITAN HYMNODY AND THE INFLUENCE OF CAMBRIDGE UNIVERSITY

Janet Wootton

During the early years of the English Reformation, and through the Civil War, the two great universities, Oxford and Cambridge, were places of lively debate and controversy. Cambridge University, in particular, produced a network of teachers and preachers, whose influence on the theology of nonconformity was considerable.

Of course, theology was not (and should never be) an isolated discipline. Radical theology grew up in dialogue with new political ideas, and the rise of rational thought, and spread into developing forms of worship and church life. The Puritan Cambridge colleges sent preachers into the churches of East Anglia and the East Midlands, and they developed networks of spiritual and practical support. After the Restoration of the monarchy (1660), when it was no longer possible to worship openly, many fled to the Netherlands, and some then to the New World, where their influence can be seen in the culture of New England and its churches.

Among the expressions of the new radical spiritual, political and theological ideas was hymnody. This was by no means straightforward. There was a huge controversy about the writing of hymns and about congregational singing, which split churches and divided communities. Nevertheless, what emerged was a tradition of plainness in music and comprehensibility in language, a combination of heartfelt worship with intellectual integrity, that has had untold influence on the culture of the English speaking world.

The Cambridge Puritans and their Concerns

In 1570, **Thomas Cartwright** (1535-1603), then newly elected Lady Margaret Professor of Divinity at Cambridge University, gave a series of lectures on the *Acts of the Apostles*. In these, he compared the organisation of the early church unfavourably with the English Church of his own day, which, though reformed, was still ruled by the pre-Reformation hierarchy of archbishops and bishops. This was at the heart of the desire for a fuller

Reformation, which would remove the layers of hierarchy in favour of a Presbyterian or even Independent tradition.

Cartwright was deprived of his chair in the furore that followed the lectures, but continued to champion the cause of greater reformation, in an open and long-running dispute with **John Whitgift** (c.1530-1604), then master of Trinity College, Cambridge, later to become Archbishop of Canterbury. On one occasion, Whitgift wrote a response to *An Admonition to the Parliament*, published anonymously in 1572, but actually by two London ministers, John Field (1545-88) and Thomas Wilcox (c.1549-1608), who each spent a year imprisoned in Newgate for their trouble. Cartwright followed immediately with a retaliation, supporting the *Admonition* and repudiating Whitgift's views.

The *Admonition* argued for 'equalitie of ministers' in church governance, but also attacked the worship of the established churches and cathedrals in mordant terms. 'Reading the service was as "evil as playing upon a stage and worse" … The reading of psalms was said to be tossed "in most places like tennis balls".'[56]

This highlights two elements of worship which were contentious and are relevant to the development of hymnody. The emphasis on the written form was seen as pernicious. Worship, in what was seen as scriptural style, should be spontaneous and Spirit-driven. The only written source was scripture itself. A great deal of the controversy surrounding hymns, as we shall see, depended on whether they were a written form of worship (which was therefore anathema) or a form of spiritual expression.

The second concern was with the professional and highly intricate form of music that had developed in the Cathedrals. The analogy with tennis is striking, and occurs again in a tract by the Independent, **Robert Browne** (d.1633):

> Their tossing to and fro of psalmes and sentences is like tenisse plaie, whereto God is called to Judg who

---

[56] Whitgift, John, *An Admonition to Parliament*, London, 1572, passim, cited in Craig, John, *The Growth of English Puritanism*, pp.34-47 in Coffey, John and Lim, Paul C.H.(Eds.), *The Cambridge Companion to Puritanism*, Cambridge University Press, Cambridge, 2008, p.39

can do best and be most gallant in his worship: as bie organs, solfaing, pricksong chanting, bussing and mumling verie roundlie on divers handes. Thus they have a shewe of religion, but in deed thei turne it to gaming, and plaie mockholidaie with the worship of God.[57]

Browne studied at Corpus Christi College, Cambridge, where he came under influence of Thomas Cartwright, among others. Plainness in music as well as in words became a characteristic of Puritan worship, and may give rise to the misconception that Puritans were somehow 'against' music itself. On the contrary, many were accomplished musicians, indeed Browne himself was a lutanist. But the requirements of worship were paramount, and both music and words should enable the heart to engage.

Behind this was a fiercely practical theology, developed, again, by Cambridge theologians such as **Richard Greenham** (early 1540s-1594), **Richard Rogers** (1551-1618) and **William Perkins** (1558-1602). Charles Hambrick-Stowe, writing on practical divinity in *The Cambridge Companion to Puritanism* considers that Richard Rogers, who sat under Greenham's preaching at Cambridge, 'may have been the first to systematise Puritanism's emerging practical divinity', through a 'life of personal spiritual and moral discipline through rigorous daily devotional practices that soon typified the Puritan way.[58]

William Perkins emerged as the greatest theologian of the Puritan movement of his time. He matriculated at Cambridge in 1577, and was also influenced by Greenham, who had established a household seminary at Dry Drayton near Cambridge. Perkins wrote *The Arte of Prophesying*, 1592 (in Latin, first English edition 1606). In a passionate, well argued and well informed treatise, he lays out the purpose and method of preaching and praying in public.

---

[57] Browne, Robert, *True and Short Declaration*, 1583, cited by Scholes, Percy A., *Oxford Companion to Music*, 3rd Edn., Oxford University Press, Oxford, 1941; ibid., *The Puritans and Music in England and New England*, 1934, reissued 1970, p.217
[58] Hambrick-Stowe, Charles E., *Practical Divinity and Spirituality*, pp.191-205 in Coffey and Lim, op. cit., p.194

To quote again from Hambrick-Stowe: 'For Perkins and other late sixteenth-century Puritans, chief among the means of grace was the Word of God preached by godly ministers of the gospel ... exegetical and evangelistic sermons painstakingly prepared for each service of worship by preachers trained in biblical scholarship and delivered in plain language that would connect with the daily lives of ordinary people.'[59]

Among other things, Perkins lists the books of the Bible with a sentence of exposition on each. He describes the Psalms as: 'sacred songs suitable for every condition of the church and its individual members, composed to be sung with grace in the heart (Col. 3:16)'[60] Again, we will see how important both applications of the Psalms, as described here, are to the development of hymnody. 'Prophesying', in Perkins' terms, is the exegesis and proclamation of the Word of God, which includes public prayer and the singing of Psalms. This formed the backbone of the network of support that developed among the godly clergy and lay people, particularly in the sphere of influence of the Cambridge Puritans.

A powerful figure in this development was the long-lived **Laurence Chaderton** (1536-1640), a moderate Puritan, and the first Master of the newly formed Emmanuel College. Emmanuel was the first college to be established after the Reformation, in 1584, by Sir Walter Mildmay (1520/21-89), as a specifically and distinctively Protestant college.[61]

Chaderton was a man of enormous influence. His students included William Perkins, and also **John Cotton** (1585-1652), who later emigrated to New England. Chaderton attended the Hampton Court Conference on 1603, one of the four Puritan representatives,

---

[59] Hambrick-Stowe, *Practical Divinity*, p.195

[60] Perkins, Richard, *The Arte of Prophesying*, Banner of Truth Trust, Carlisle, 1996, reprinted 2011, p.14

[61] http://www.emma.cam.ac.uk/about/history/college/, accessed 20/05/14. The website notes that 'In the 1630's, many Puritan clergy went into exile to avoid persecution. Of the first 100 graduates who migrated to New England fully one third were Emmanuel men. Cambridge in Massachusetts was named in compliment to an Emmanuel preacher, Thomas Shepherd; another, John Harvard (BA 1632), emigrated in 1637. He died the following year and left his books and half his estate to the new college that was thus to bear his name and become the first American University.'

meeting with King James I and VI, and the Church of England Bishops. He also headed the team translating *1 Chronicles* to the *Song of Songs*, for the King James Version of the Bible.

Under Chaderton Emmanuel College was instrumental in providing godly clergy to the parishes of Eastern and Central England. These men formed a 'spiritual brotherhood of preachers, mostly graduates of the University of Cambridge, where their undergraduate careers overlapped, who went on to minister in London, Essex and East Anglia.'[62] Their meetings took the form of 'prophesyings', 'intense, ideologically motivated sessions' which 'reflect both the secrecy and zeal of a reformist and potentially revolutionary group.'[63] Interestingly, the gatherings were to a certain extent egalitarian. The hearers were expected to use spiritual discernment to judge the spirituality and authenticity of the speaker, as in 1 Corinthians 14:29. This was a sphere in which, controversially, the voices of women could occasionally be released, albeit probably not in the meetings which developed under the aegis of colleges like Emmanuel.[64]

Although the meetings for learning and support were suppressed in Elizabethan England, they continued, and seem to have provided early opportunities for newly trained ministers to preach, and find their way into pastorates. Tom Webster writes: 'These exercises formed an entrance into a network of advancement and recognition of the godly in the university and beyond, and put at the disposal of the young cleric a resource of professional and religious advice ... It became axiomatic that a minister could return to Cambridge to take advantage of this resource.' Furthermore, '... for godly students at a later stage of development, such connections afforded early

---

[62] Haller, W., *The Rise of Puritanism or, The Way to the New Jerusalem as Set Forth in Pulpit and Press from Thomas Cartwright to John Lilburne and John Milton, 1570-1643*, Harper Torchbooks, New York, NY, 1938, reprinted 1957, pp.49-82, cited in Keeble, N.H., *Puritanism and Literature*, pp.309-326 in Coffey and Lim (Eds.), op. cit., p.320

[63] Rolph, R.S., *Emmanuel College Cambridge and the Puritan Movements*, PhD Thesis, University of Southern California, Los Angeles, CA, 1979

[64] See Wiseman, Susan, *Women's poetry*, pp.127-147; Wilcox, Helen and Ottway, Sheila, *Women's histories*, pp.148-161; and Horby, Elaine, *Prophecy, enthusiasm and female pamphleteers*, pp.162-179 in Keeble, N.H., *The Cambridge Companion to the Writing of the English Revolution*, Cambridge University Press, Cambridge, 2001.

opportunities to preach, as students and tutors provided villages around Cambridge and further afield with regular sermons.'[65]

The last thread in this pattern is the one that links worship, spirituality, life and politics, and it runs through another Cambridge College, Sidney Sussex. Famous as the college attended by **Oliver Cromwell** (1599-1658), it 'offered a sound Protestant upbringing, the Master and Fellows being required by the Statutes to abhor "Popery and all heresies, superstitions and errors".'[66] Cromwell went up to Sidney Sussex in 1616, and the college boasts among its students 'a number of early pioneering colonists in America such as the poetical George Moxon and Cromwell's footballing friend John Wheelwright; and Sir John Reynolds, one of Cromwell's finest soldiers who died shipwrecked on Goodwin Sands.'[67]

But it is a series of lectures on Roman history to which I want to draw attention, given in 1627 by the Dutch Calvinist, **Isaac Dorislaus** (1595-1649), first holder of a new chair of history at Cambridge, appointed by the Puritan Lord Brooke. The problem was that a study of the Roman Republic could be used to denounce monarchy and support the classical model of government: '... there were dangers inherent in Tacitus' political discourse: his discussions of republican government, of civil liberty, and of resistance to tyranny had inspired republican and resistance theorists from Bruni and Machiavelli to Lipsius and Buchanan.'[68]

The chair of history did not survive, as, 'the teaching of history had proved too great a threat to monarchy for it to be sanctioned by the upholders of the early Stuart establishment.'[69] Just as Cartwright's

---

[65] Webster, Tom, *Godly Clergy in Early Stuart England: The Caroline Puritan Movement, 1620-1643*, Cambridge University Press, Cambridge, 1997, pp.21, 23

[66] Rogers, Nicholas and Parish Christopher, *Cromwell and Sidney Sussex*, Sidney Sussex College, Cambridge, 1999), p.1

[67] https://www.sid.cam.ac.uk/aboutus/visitors/history.html, accessed 20/05/14. Actually, the website does not 'boast' these scholars but seems rather reluctant to show its Puritan colours.

[68] Todd, Margo, *Anti-Calvinists and the Republican Threat in Early Stuart Cambridge*, pp.85-105 in Knoppers, Laura Lunger (Ed.), *Puritanism and its Discontents*, Associated University Presses, London, 2003), p.86

[69] ibid., p.93

1577 lectures on *Acts* had questioned the rights of bishops and archbishops to rule the Church, so Dorilaus' (and others') work on Tacitus and the Roman Republic laid the ground for calling the King to account, and even for regicide. Henceforward the intellectual stage was being set for revolution and civil war.

Hymns and Psalms

The principles of Puritan practical theology focus on the centrality of the Bible; the access of every person to salvation through faith alone; plainness in living and in worship; an intolerance of super-imposed hierarchy or leadership, with a concomitant requirement that leaders are accountable to the people. These emerged in a style of worship that tested everything by reference to the Bible as authority and the Spirit of God as inspiration. All written forms of worship were seen as lifeless. Worship should be a spontaneous response to the words of Scripture as interpreted and proclaimed in 'prophesying', the Spirit-inspired words of the preacher.

What if the same principles were applied to singing in worship? The singing of Psalms (as opposed to reading them as Scripture) and, later, hymns, was beset by controversy on all sides. In the first place, the Psalms were written forms of worship and therefore could be seen as 'formal' and spiritless, like the written prayers and formal liturgy that godly Christians so despised. As Scripture, they were sacrosanct, but questions arose about their use for congregational worship. Furthermore, if they were to be sung, there were serious questions about the form in which they were used: in translation, certainly, but could their Hebrew verse form be translated into English metre as well? And then, was there any warrant for the use of English melodies to carry the metre?

The New Testament referred to 'new song' (Revelation 5:9), and many argued that, if there were to be singing, it should be spontaneous and arise from the spiritual gift of an individual; more like extempore prayer, or speaking in tongues than reading written words. This would take the form of an inspired individual singing, with the congregation responding with an 'Amen' if the words met with their approval (as discerners of the Spirit, 1 Corinthians 12:10).

Finally, while the separate singing of priests and choirs was rejected, congregational singing was also suspect. Again, it smacked of 'formal' worship, in which 'ungodly' congregations recited words by rote. The singing of a 'mixed' congregation might contravene the restriction on women's voices being heard in church (1 Corinthians 14:34-35); and words that should be sung only by the godly, with grace in their hearts, might also involve unbelievers, on whose lips the songs would be heretical.[70]

However, there were early attempts to provide versified settings of the Psalms for congregational singing. The central overriding aim was to make this great corpus of worship and poetry in the Bible as accessible as possible to ordinary worshipping people, so that they could sing with their heart and their understanding in worship of God. This meant that adherence to the original text overrode considerations of taste or beauty in words or music, and that every adaptation had to be argued for, in terms of accessibility.

Henry Ainsworth (1569-1622) was a Hebrew scholar, educated first at St John's and later at Caius College, Cambridge. His *Book of Psalmes Englished both in Prose and in Metre* was published while he was in exile in the Netherlands. The title page bears a quotation from Ephesians 5:18-19: 'Be yee filled with the Spirit, speaking to yourselves in Psalms, Hymns, and spirituall Songs: singing and making melodie in your hearts to the Lord.' Its preface gives fascinating insight into the dilemmas faced by the translator and versifier in this context.

Ainsworth sets the Psalms in prose as well as poetry, '[f]or the better discerning thereof[71] and adds commentary. He finds he has to compromise a little in the metrical versions, for example, inserting the word 'thankfully' in Psalm 103:1-2, 'whereas in prose, I use only *blesse*, but the scripture proveth *thanks* to be included in our *blessing* of God ...' and he goes on to give a detailed scriptural example of the use of the two words. Similarly, he argues for the use of rhyme as an English convention, on the basis that the original texts make use of the poetic conventions of Hebrew. Yet,

[70] Isaac Marlow, *The Controversie of Singing brought to an End*, London, 1692
[71] Henry Ainsworth, *The Booke of Psalmes: Englished both in prose and metre*, Amsterdam, 1612, p.A 2

he says, 'rather than I would stray from the text, I straine now and then, with rules of our English poesie ... which in a work of this sort, I trust all sincere minded will forgive.'[72]

As to tunes, he writes, 'I find none set of God: so that each people is to use the most grave, decent, and comfortable manner of singing that they know, according to this generall rule; 1 Corinthians 14,26.40.'[73] On this principle, he selects English, French and Dutch tunes, the first 'when they will fit the measure of the verse', and the last two 'for the other long verses'.[74] The English tunes tend to be common metre.

In fact, he is quite adventurous in his choice of metres. His 'Psalm 23' reads as follows (the numbers referring to the Psalm verses):

> [1] Iehovah feedeth me, I shall not lack.
> [2] In grassy fields, he down doth make me lye:
> he gently-leads me, quiet waters by.
> [3] He doth return my soul: for his name sake,
> in paths of justice leads-me-quietly.
>
> [4] Yea though I walk, in dale of deadly shade,
> ile fear none ill; for with me thou *wilt be:*
> thy rod thy staff eke, they shall comfort me.
> [5] Fore me, a table thou hast ready-made;
> in their presence that my distressers be:
>
> Thou makest fat mine head with ointing oil;
> my cup abounds. [6] Doubtless good and mercy
> shall all the dayes of my life follow me:
> also within Iehovahs house I shall
> to length of dayes, repose me quietly.

This is by no means an easy metre or rhyme scheme, and yet, with one exception, in verse 3 line 2, stress and scansion are good. Caesuras are often marked with punctuation, but are sometimes cleverly varied, as in verse 1 line 1 and verse 2 line 1. The

---

[72] ibid., p.A 2
[73] ibid., p.A 3
[74] ibid., p.A 3

repetition of 'quiet' and 'quietly', the latter at the end of the first and last verses, is effective, where the feeling of the line declines with the tune; and there are some nice touches, such as the alliteration 'dale of deadly shade' in verse 2.

The tune note refers the singer to Psalm 8, where the stately tune, OLD 124TH from the Genevan Psalter of 1551 is laid out. He does set Psalm 124 to this tune as well, but less successfully.

There are many references to the dullness of Puritan psalmody, but I can imagine singing this version of Psalm 23 in a congregation, with a real sense of movement through the text, as an integral part of a service. This is described in the *Cambridge Companion to Puritanism*: 'The drama played out within Puritan services of worship involved the interplay of scriptural themes and images building upon one another in sung psalter sections, spoken prayers, a biblical text read aloud and the preached Word based on that text.'[75]

In 1934 Percy Scholes described it more passionately:

> The gorgeous Hebrew poetry was set to melodies that expressed it adequately, provided the heart was there from which the response could come – and it was! The thoughts of joy and lamentation, of confidence and of triumph over one's enemies (who were, of course, at the same time God's enemies) were so much in keeping with Puritan feeling, in a day when persecution had been long endured and might still be renewed, that if some Puritan genius had been at hand to cast the emotions of the seventeenth-century Puritan community into original verse, he could not have come closer to its intimate expression than did the age-old Psalms. They therefore enrolled David as a Puritan![76]

---

[75] Hambrick-Stowe, *Practical Divinity*, p.200
[76] Como, David R., *Radical Puritanism, c.1558-1660*, pp.241-258 in Coffey and Lim, op.cit., pp.253-254

Ainsworth's book endured for the next thirty years, and was the only musical resource taken by the exiles on the Mayflower to the Plymouth colony in New England, where it was used for a generation. The 1629-30 settlers carried '*Sternhold and Hopkins*',[77] which they criticised not for its poetry but for its lack of faithfulness to the text and meaning of the Hebrew psalms. The first book to be printed in New England was an attempt to create an accurate rendering of the Psalms in English verse, the Bay Psalm Book of 1640. This versification removed most of the more complex metres of Ainsworth's collection, in favour of CM, DCM, SM or LM. Thus the 23rd Psalm begins:

> The Lord to mee a shepherd is,
> Want therefore shall not I.
> Hee in the folds of tender grasse
> Doth cause mee down to lie:

Richard Watson calls it 'a text that demonstrates the Puritan preference for plain speech in an extreme form.'[78] He cites the Preface, now thought to be by John Cotton: 'If therefore the verses are not always so smooth and elegant as some may desire or expect; let them consider that God's Altar needs no polishings: Ex. 20, for we have respected rather a plaine translation, than to smooth our verses with the sweetnes of any paraphrase, and soe have attended Conscience rather than Elegance, fidelity rather than poetry.'[79]

Cotton had been at Trinity College, Cambridge, and later at Emmanuel, where he came under the influence of Laurence Chaderton and William Perkins, among others. He was already a pre-eminent preacher and theologian when he was forced to flee to New England in 1633, in his middle years. He was the most prominent of the English clergy to go to New England, and did a great deal to establish the theology and practice of the colony.

---

[77] Sternhold, T., Hopkins, J., et al, *The Whole Booke of Psalmes, Collected into English Meter*, John Day, 1562, reprinted Company of Stationers, London, 1720

[78] Watson, J.R, *The English Hymn: a Critical and Historical Study*, Clarendon Press, Oxford, 1997) p.108

[79] Preface to the *Bay Psalm Book*, 1639-40, cited in Watson, op. cit., p.100, n.13

His influence on the lives of the churches and their worship can be seen on both sides of the Atlantic. In later years, his grandson, ⌐ **Cotton Mather** (1663-1728), commented that 'Immanuel College contributed more than a little' to make New England 'in some respects Immanuel's Land',[80] and indeed John Harvard (1607-38), whose benefaction made possible the establishment of Harvard College in Cambridge, Mass. in 1636, was also an Emmanuel graduate.

Cotton was influential in the Westminster Assembly, although by the time it met he was in New England, and the 1644 *Westminster Directory for the Public Worship of God Throughout the Three Kingdomes of England, Scotland and Wales* comes down quite clearly on the side of congregational singing. The document calls the singing of Psalms an 'ordinance' that is, a practice ordained by Jesus, parallel to Baptism and Communion, which are also known as ordinances, rather than sacraments. On days of thanksgiving, 'because the singing of Psalmes is of all other the most proper Ordinance for expressing Joy and Thanksgiving, let some pertinent Psalme or Psalmes be sung for that purpose.'[81] As such it becomes 'the duty of Christians to praise God publicly by singing of Psalmes together in the Congregation, and also privately in the family', though 'the chief care must be, to sing with understanding and with grace in the heart, making melody unto the Lord.'[82]

At the same time as the Westminster Assembly was sitting, Cotton produced *The Way of the Churches of Christ* in New England in 1645 and a treatise on worship, *Singing of Psalmes, A Gospel-Ordinance or Treatise*, in 1650. The former book records the practice of the churches: 'Before Sermon and many times after, we sing a Psalme", and what must be a 'reference to the *Bay Psalm Book*, "because the former translation of the Psalmes, doth in many things vary from the Original ... we have endeavoured a new

---

[80] Mather, Cotton, *Magnalia Christi Americana or The Ecclesiastical History of New England*, 1852; reprinted, Russell and Russell, New York, NY, 1967, p.355, cited in Pointer, Steven, *The Emmanuel College, Cambridge, Election of 1622: The Constraints of a Puritan Institution*, pp.106-121 in Knoppers (Ed.), op. cit., p.108
[81] *Directory for the Publick Worship of God Throughout the Three Kingdomes of England, Scotland and Wales*, London, 164, p.38
[82]. ibid., p.40

translation into English meetre, as neere the originall as wee could express it in our English tongue.'[83]

Cotton, then, like the authors of the *Directory*, is in favour of congregational singing, and he explores the controversies surrounding the practice in the later treatise on *Singing of Psalmes*, which makes its position quite clear in the title: *A Gospel Ordinance*. The introduction lays out the areas of controversy to be covered:

1. Touching the Duty it selfe
2. Touching the Matter to be Sung
3. Touching the Singers
4. Touching the Manner of Singing[84]

To the first two matters, his response is that the singing of Psalms is an ordinance, not merely permitted, but commanded by God during worship. Then he moves on to the singers and the manner of singing, and here some important principles of non-conformist singing emerge. The singers, he is quite clear, are to be all the members of a congregation, or even any gathering of people in any place. He deals with the exception of women relatively briefly, by noting that by singing it cannot be assumed that women are teaching or asking questions, which are the two forms of speaking most specifically proscribed (1 Corinthians 14:34-35).

As to unbelievers, Cotton argues that the ordinance extends to every person. Just as all people are enjoined to pray, when in trouble or thanksgiving, so '*Travellers, Prisoners, Sickmen, Seamen*, being saved from severall distresses by the good hand of the Lord, they are all of them commanded *to praise the Lord for his goodnesse*, and to *declare his wonders before the sonnes of men*, Psal. 107.6. to 32.'[85]

By this means, he suggests, the singers themselves may be convicted of their unbelief: 'the end of singing is not onely to

---

[83] Cotton, John, *The Way of the Churches of Christ in New England*, Matthew Simmons, London, 1645, p.67
[84] Cotton, John, *Singing of Psalmes, A Gospel-Ordinance*, J. Rothwell & H. Allen, London, 1650, p.1
[85] ibid., p.45

instruct, and admonish, and comfort the upright, but also to instruct, and convince, and reprove the wicked, as hath been shewed, Deut. 31.19.'[86] This is an important point. Unexpectedly, in a form of worship that can become inward looking, the gathered church of godly believers, worrying about the ungodly in their midst, Cotton sees the singing of Psalms in worship as a missionary activity. The terminology may be anachronistic, but here is a glimpse of the sentiment!

There is no place for a choir or select group of singers: 'If God has reserved this Dutie to some select Choristers, he would have given some direction in the *New Testament* for their Qualification and Election: But since he speaketh nothing of any such select Musicians, he commendeth this Dutie to the whole Church.'[87]

The last section of the treatise turns to the translation of the Psalms, not only into the English language but also into English verse. The argument is fascinating, and confronts issues that face translators of hymnody in our own time. Firstly, he contends that it is appropriate to translate the form as well as the language: 'If then it be the holy will of God, that the Hebrew Scriptures should be translated into English Prose in order unto reading, then it is in like sort his holy will, that the Hebrew Psalmes, (which are Poems and Verses) should be translated into English Poems and Verses in order to Singing.'[88] This makes 'the Verses more easie for memory, and more fit for melody.'[89] Then, in contradiction to the usual reticence about beauty or elegance, he writes:

> to express the elegancy of the Originall language in translation ... Yea doubtless it were a part of the due Faithfulnesse in a Translator, as to declare the whole Counsell of God, word for word; so to expresse lively every elegancy of the Holy Ghost, (as much as the vulgar language can reach) that so the People of God

---

[86] ibid., p.48
[87] ibid., p.39
[88] ibid., p.55
[89] ibid., p.55

may be kindly affected, as well with the manner, as with the matter of the Holy Scriptures.[90]

The translation pays attention not only to elegance, as a matter of honouring God, but also to the emotional force of the original texts. This runs counter to the usual dismissal of ornament or beauty, which is seen as a distraction from the plain, unvarnished meaning of the Psalms.

Wilderness and War

Behind the sophistication of this discussion lies the raw emotional power of the Psalms, which suited the Puritan mindset and experience very well. The early emigrations to Holland and the New World were set against the backdrop of persecution, civil war, regicide and commonwealth in England. They were intense and violent times, and created an intense and powerful literature.

John Milton (1608-1674), who graduated from Christ's College, Cambridge in 1629, wrote brilliant and scathing political prose, as well as visionary poetry, attacking the conformist clergy, defending and providing a rationale for Puritan and radical ideals. David Loewenstein argues that:

> Scholars have sometimes divorced the writer of occasional, fiercely polemical tracts during the Revolution from the visionary author of sublime, lofty poetry. The two, poet and revolutionary polemicist, were, however, closely connected. Milton contributed actively – and imaginatively – to the vital textual dimension of the English Revolution.[91]

Milton's prose was frequently acerbic, and illustrates very well the charged nature of the times. But it also builds a visionary landscape, bringing the conflict into lively dialogue with the Scriptures. Like Dorislaus, he also draws on the ideal of the Roman Republic for a political model which is not a monarchy, and

---

[90] ibid., p.56

[91] David Loewenstein, *Milton's Prose and the Revolution*, pp87-106 in Keeble, N.H. (Ed.), *The Cambridge Companion to Writing of the English Revolution*, Cambridge University Press, Cambridge, 2001, p.87

his allusions are classical as well as biblical. In Scripture, he finds inspiration in the mighty battles of the Apocalypse, in the wars over the Promised Land, and (in the dying days of the republic) in the release from slavery in Egypt.[92]

The impact of the Civil War on the people of England was enormous. During its bloody years, a higher proportion of the population was killed than in the First World War. Both sides turned to the Bible, and particularly to the Hebrew Scriptures, not only for the justification of their position, but also for the spiritual nourishment of their aims. N.H. Keeble, editor of *The Cambridge Companion to Puritanism*, draws parallels with Milton and Bunyan as well as with hymnwriters such as Benjamin Keach (1640-1704), in his essay on *Puritanism and Literature*:

> ... the Puritan imagination was especially responsive to the narratives of the many historical battles and migrations through which God guides his chosen people Israel in the Old Testament and to the Bible's many metaphorical deployments of warfare and of wayfaring ... Its preferred images and narrative patterns derive from journeying and combat, itinerancy and warfare.[93]

In public worship and private devotion, this meant turning to the Psalms, and their influence was popular, democratic and incalculable. In the New Model Army, organised by Oliver Cromwell, and in the communities it from which it drew, worship took on a greater sense of urgency. The fight against tyranny played out in spiritual life in a fierce protection of freedom in worship. As John Morrill writes, 'By mid 1647 a high proportion of the officers and troopers of the New Model Army had experienced, and were committed to, free forms of worship in which anyone could break open the scripture and lead their contemporaries in free prayer.'[94]

---

[92] See Loewenstein, Milton's Prose and the Revolution, passim.

[93] Keeble, N.H., *Puritanism and Literature*, pp.309-326 in Coffey and Lim, op. cit., p.317

[94] Morrill, John, *The Puritan Revolution*, pp.67-88 in Coffey and Lim, op. cit., p.74

The Psalms became the battle songs of the war, providing a ready supply of warlike texts, to celebrate victory over the enemy, and lament defeat and death. They were the ringing battle cries of people and tribes beset by enemies, falling in defeat or rising in triumph. The very militaristic imagery that we find so difficult to deal with in more liberal and peaceful times gave vivid expression to a people who felt they were fighting for God. David Wykes notes, 'the language of the Old Testament, with its war-like imagery and relentless onslaught against God's foes, suited seventeenth-century Puritans admirably, particularly during the Civil War when Parliament's enemies were seen as God's as well.'[95]

Cromwell resorted to the Psalms at crucial times in his career. Most famously, following the spectacular victory at Dunbar, where Cromwell defeated an army more than twice the size of his own, he ordered the singing of Psalm 117, a two-verse shout of triumph and praise. Horton Davies cites R.E. Prothero: 'It was but a brief respite. Practical in his religion as in all else, Cromwell chose the shortest psalm in the book.'[96]

They infiltrated the language and thinking of the period: 'One could well believe that the Psalms were the iron-rations of Cromwell's Ironsides, so thoroughly was their chief commander's thought and vocabulary nourished on them ... he cited from them at the most dramatic stages of his career, while in his public despatches and private letters, as in his speeches before Parliament, he made their phraseology entirely his own.'[97]

Following the Restoration of the Monarchy in 1660, nonconformists moved from warfare to persecution, worshipping in small, secret groups, constantly on the watch for betrayal. Now they had moved

---

[95] Wykes, David, *From David's Psalms to Watts's Hymns: the Development of Hymnody among Dissenters Following the Toleration Act*, pp.227-239 in Swanson, R.N. (Ed.), *Continuity and Change in Christian Worship*, Boydell Press, Woodbridge, 1999, p.230

[96] Davies, Horton, *Worship and Theology in England*, vol. II, *From Andrewes to Baxter and Fox, 1603-1690*,: Princeton University Press, Princeton, NJ, 1975, p.270, citing Prothero, R.E. (Lord Ernle), *The Psalms in Human Life*, John Murray, London, 1904, p.194

[97] Davies, *Worship and Theology in England*, vol. II, p.270, drawing on Prothero, *Psalms in Human Life*, p.189

from war to wilderness, and again found a rich resource for worship in the Hebrew Scriptures. But hymn singing as a regular part of worship had to wait for the relative peace of the Act of Toleration in 1689. Then, at last, it was possible to establish regular worship and organise and maintain congregational life.

This hymnody that emerged at the end of the seventeenth and beginning of the eighteenth century was imbued with the themes of wilderness that continued to characterise nonconformist life. Though 'tolerated', nonconformists were still excluded from civic and educational institutions. The choice to remain true to dissent was a choice that precluded advancement through normal channels.

The poignant poem by **Richard Baxter** (1615-91), which has come into modern hymnody through the selection that normally starts: 'He wants not friends that hath thy love', carries the sorrowfulness of the ejection itself. Earthly life is seen as a voyage over a tempestuous ocean, with the haven beckoning.[98] Other hymns of his that are still in use describe life in terms of the lost and wandering sheep, or a journey through dark rooms.[99]

The Welsh hymnwriter **William Williams** of Pantycelyn (1717-1791) came from nonconformist roots, but took orders within the established Church in Wales. However, he became involved in the Methodist revival, and was refused entry to the priesthood. His hymns, published in Welsh in collections from 1744 onwards. Here, the language of wilderness draws in the sombre landscape of his native land.

Alan Gaunt's (b.1935) recent translations have brought some of these to new light. Texts such as:

> A pilgrim in a desert land
> I wander and I roam,
> Almost expecting every hour
> To reach my Father's home.[100]

---

[98] Baxter, Richard, 'He wants not friends that hath thy love', v3

[99] Baxter, Richard, 'Christ who knows all his sheep'; 'Lord, it belongs not to my care', v3

[100] Williams, William, 'Pererin wyf mewn anial dir', tr. Gaunt, Alan

bear out the sense of a brooding landscape, which is best known to us through various versions of his 'Arglwydd, arwain trwy'r anialwch': 'Guide me, O Thou great Jehovah, / Pilgrim through this barren land ...' with all its references to the journey of the people of Israel through the wilderness: the stream of water; and the pillar of cloud and fire.

The writer who truly provides a bridge from the psalmody of the Civil War to the hymnody of our own time is of course **Isaac Watts** (1674-1748). Watts was born into dissent and chose to remain true to it. His texts provide the sung theology of nonconformity taking shape during the Enlightenment. Many are highly sophisticated explorations of the Christian's relation to God, who is the infinite unknown,[101] while others hark back to the radical language of the dissenters in dangerous times.

He is very clear that the gathered people at worship are the 'saints': 'Jesus invites his saints / To meet around his board ... ' and that they are saints because of God's grace, not through their own merits: 'Here pardon'd rebels sit and hold / Communion with their Lord.'[102]

Daniel Ritchie comments that 'When congregations sang Watts' lyrics of the "saints" ... their language reflected the tribal rhetoric of seventeenth-century Puritanism.' This language was actually helping to create the identity of dissent, from the images of the previous generation, looking to the Old Testament for their 'national myth' rather than to 'consecrated version of the Tudor royal history as found in Shakespeare'. [103] The 'saints' are under God's protection, and, in the intensely political hymn, 'Our God, our help in ages past' they are under the shadow of God's throne, and kept by his sure defence.

---

[101] Watts, Isaac, 'God is a name my soul adores', v1
[102] Watts, Isaac, 'Jesus invites his saints', v1
[103] Ritchie, Daniel E., *The Fullness of Knowing: Modernity and Postmodernity from Defoe to Gadamer*, Baylor University Press, Waco, TX, 2010, p.50

Old and New Worlds

Watts' hymns held sway for a generation on both sides of the Atlantic. In the 'New World' they entered into dialogue with the experience of the colonists, and with other American communities. **Jonathan Edwards** (1703-58) prized Watts' texts and even suggested that they lay behind the early Spiritual Awakening, as Mark Noll comments: 'his paradigm-making account of the 1734-35 revival in Northampton, Massachusetts, specified hymn-singing as a key element of this awakening.'[104] Edwards' grandson, **Timothy Dwight** (1752-1817), then President of Yale, produced a revised and enlarged collection of Watts' hymns[105] in 1801 at the instigation of the General Association of Connecticut. In addition to revised texts of Watts, he included thirty-three of his own hymns.

I have explored the development of the wilderness theme in an article, *The Wilderness and Christian Song*.[106] The New Englanders saw their journey and settlement of the land very much in Old Testament terms, as a journey through the wilderness to the Promised Land. But the language of the nineteenth century hymns evokes a strange sense of loss, as if the Promised Land is still a distant, even receding hope.

I have also commented on Dwight's text, 'I love thy kingdom, Lord', which is arguably 'the American hymn which has remained in longest continuous use'.[107] It is a setting of Psalm 137, a Psalm of wilderness lament, which indeed carries over into the hymn text. The text carries a sense of loss and yearning: 'For her my tears shall fall, / for her my prayers ascend'.

---

[104] Noll, Mark A., *The Defining Role of Hymns in Early Evangelicalism*, pp.3-16 in Mouw, Richard J. & Noll, Mark A. (Eds.), *Wonderful words of life: Hymns in American Protestant history and theology*, Eerdmans Publishing Co., Grand Rapids, MI, 2004, pp.4-5, citing Edwards, *A Faithful Narrative of the Surprising Work of God*, 1737

[105] Dwight, Timothy (Ed.), *The Psalms of David, &c.... By I. Watts, D.D. A New Edition in which the Psalms omitted by Dr. Watts are versified, local passages are altered, and a number of Psalms are versified anew in proper metres. By Timothy Dwight, D.D., &c....To the Psalms is added a Selection of Hymns, Hudson & Godwin, New Haven, CT, 1801*

[106] Wootton, Janet, *The Wilderness and Christian Song*, Lecture given at the Seventh Congregational Symposium of the NACCC at Olivet, October 28-30, 2010, and published in *International Congregational Journal*, 10.1, Spring 2011, pp.75-90

[107] Biography of Timothy Dwight, in *HymnQuest*, 2014

This seems strange in a hymn written in the aftermath of the American Revolution, when surely paraphrases of praise Psalms might be more appropriate. However, Rochelle Stackhouse notes that the period around the Revolution was religiously more unstable than we might think, at least from outside the United States.[108]

The hymns of Watts and the evocative texts of Pantycelyn were also taken up among the African slaves on American plantations, another wilderness indeed. Giovan Venable King explores two versions of Watts' text, 'I love the Lord who heard my cries' in *The African American Heritage Hymnal*.[109] The text is set to two tunes, an 'African-American traditional tune,' arranged in 1975 by the well-known gospel artist Richard Smallwood, and another, listed as a 'Meter hymn, anonymous; lined out by M. Adams and Louis Sykes.' Both tunes have characteristics that link the text to its use among African slave communities: in the first, for example, 'There is a drop from a D to an F in the melody of the last line. This is a drop to a minor 6th, very common in African music, but relatively rare in European-style music'.[110]

But it is in the text that King finds the reason for the hymn's appeal to a people in wilderness, with its evidence of real human suffering, in the life of the writer:

> I love the Lord, who heard my cries
> And pitied every groan.
> Long as I live when troubles rise,
> I'll hasten to God's throne.[111]

Perhaps for the same reasons, the hymns of Pantycelyn resonate with African American hymnody. 'Guide me, O thou great Jehovah'

---

[108] Wootton, 'The Wilderness and Christian Song', pp.86-87, citing Stackhouse, Rochelle A., *Hymnody and Politics: Isaac Watts's 'Our God, Our Help in Ages Past' and Timothy Dwight's 'I Love Thy Kingdom, Lord'*, pp.42-66 in Mouw & Noll, op. cit. p.65
[109] *The African-American Heritage Hymnal*, GIA Publications, Inc., Chicago, IL, 2001), nos.394, 395
[110] King, Giovan Venable, *Psalms in the Key of Life: Isaac Watts and the Composers of Negro Spirituals*, pp.41-58 in *International Congregational Journal*, 4.2, February 2005, pp.50-51
[111] Watts, Isaac, 'I love the Lord who heard my cries'

is set to an anonymous American tune called ARISE,[112] which gives the song, as Martin Tel says, a 'context of honest lament', absent in the triumphalist CWM RHONDDA.

George McCue has brought together a collection of articles tracing the influence of Puritan hymnody right through to modern American culture in his book, *Music in American Society 1776-1976*. In it, Kenneth Phillips explores the influence of Watts' hymns through the slave communities on twentieth-century African American music, to create a style that became the voice of the civil rights movement.[113] The same themes of campaign, wilderness and promise still ring true.

Similarly the influence of Puritan hymnody can be heard in both black and white fundamentalist churches across America, but, as Austin Caswell notes, writing in the same collection, 'we are uncomfortable with our heritage of hymnody', since middle-class Americans aspire to 'become more like their image of the sophisticated European and less like their image of the bumpkins who populated the United States.'[114]

The same is true on this side of the Atlantic. The songs of Watts were joined by the powerful texts of the Wesleyan revival, drawing on a now well established tradition of popular religious song. Right through the nineteenth century, hymns and other forms of popular song were great shapers of people's thinking. Campaign songs carried the messages of social reform into the consciousness of vast gatherings around the abolition of the slave trade; the Sunday Schools movement; temperance; women's emancipation. They formed the rallying cries of the new socialist movement. Jane

---

[112] James, E. Wyn, *Welsh Ballads and American Slavery*, http://www.cardiff.ac.uk/insrv/ libraries/scolar/digital/welshballads/welsh-ballads-and-american-slavery.html#_ednref6 accessed 11/10/10; Tel, Martin Tel, *Hymns to mark the journey of God's people*, *Reformed Worship*, 80, http://www.reformedworship.org/magazine/article.cfm? article_id=1691 accessed 11/10/10

[113] Billups, Kenneth B., *The Other Side of Black Music*, pp.87-94 in McCue, George, *Music in American Society 1776-1976: From Puritan Hymn to Synthesizer*, Transaction Books, New Brunswick, NJ, 1977

[114] Caswell, Austin B., *Social and Moral Music: The Hymn*, pp.47-72 in McCue, op. cit., p.48

70

Addams, visiting from Chicago, recalls an occasion at the Mansfield Settlement in East London, when 'we heard Keir Hardie, before a large audience of working-men standing in the open square of Canning Town, outline the great things to be accomplished by the then new Labor Party, and we joined the vast body of men in the booming hymn, "When wilt Thou save the people, O God of Mercy, when!"'[115]

The Great Awakenings swept across the Atlantic, and a tide of writing for mission grew up as the missionary societies were formed in the 1790's, to carry the gospel around the world in in the footsteps of explorers and empire-builders. Missionaries on furlough spoke to great congregations, who sang their support, often in what now sound excruciatingly racist and paternalistic hymns. In the mission 'field', evangelistic songs were translated as fervently as the Bible, into local indigenous languages, and often sung to tunes and using instruments that were wildly out of keeping with local culture. Nevertheless, these hymns are still sung and loved in many parts of the world, as much part of the culture now as the Christian world music that is beginning to arise.

Hymnody has been unjustly ignored by commentators on literature and culture. The form is still very sparsely studied, despite its huge cultural and societal impact. Words set to music, and sung by great congregations, or in family worship, formed the thinking, and not just the thinking, but the emotions, the aims and dreams, of generations. The emphasis of the Cambridge Puritans (among others) on plain and understandable words, expressing an intensely practical theology, and set to accessible music to be sung by whole congregations, created a form of popular song that has had an untold influence on the world in which we live.

---

[115] Addams, Jane, *Twenty Years at Hull House with Autobiographical Notes,* Macmillan, New York, NY, 1911, pp.263-264, cited in Wootton, Janet and Isherwood, Lisa (Eds.), *The Spirit of Dissent: Commemorations of the Great Ejectment of 1662,* Institute of Theological Partnerships, Winchester, forthcoming

THE LIVING TRADITION

Christopher Idle

It was C.S. Lewis, that essentially Oxford man who in 1954 moved to Cambridge to take up the newly founded chair of Mediaeval and Renaissance Literature, who told Dr Erik Routley that what we need are better, shorter and fewer hymns; 'especially fewer'.

Cambridge has made a distinctive contribution towards the 'better'; some have produced what are 'shorter', compared with much that had gone before; but it might be said it has done little to promote the 'fewer'.

Our approximate starting point is *The Cambridge Hymnal* of 1967. In sketching some of the Cambridge characters since then, and some whose work both preceded and followed it, we find Ridley Hall as a common factor in fourteen of them. Is there something about this place, close to the centre, peculiarly conducive to the love of hymns?   Its first Principal was the hymn-writing Bishop Handley Moule (1841-1920); could a tradition bear fruit from such late nineteenth-century seeds?

But the space is apportioned here between those whose known output is modest, others who have written several hymns, and those whose texts reach three figures spanning several decades. Further sections cover hymnologists and composers, but the boundaries are flexible. The order of names in these sections is that of their birth-dates; 'Cambridge' includes those who have significantly studied, taught, lived or worked here.

No assumptions are made about quality; the relative length of the entries is no guide to their perceived merit. Some Cambridge figures seem to endure hymns as part of the 'church music' package; others become involved with tunes through their prime concern with texts. Blessed are they who show equal regard for words and music! Hymn-lovers accept that some fine verses have not resonated with Sunday congregations, whereas compositions of more limited skill prove a means of grace to millions.

Hymns are distinguished here from 'worship-songs', in consisting of two or more regular stanzas designed for congregations rather than choir, music-group or solo use; like creeds or confessions they are 'stand-alone', unrepeated items, and the text may have more than one tune. Most words are written by someone other than the composer.

The Cambridge Hymnal

Anyone coming to *The Cambridge Hymnal* fresh after half a century could find it enigmatic. Its plan – numbers 1-139 alphabetically, forty for Christmas and a postscript of fifteen – seems to rule it out as a congregational compilation. So do the footnotes translating the Latin or glossing an archaism. The hymnal might even serve to embody the C.S. Lewis programme: quality, brevity and paucity.

For quality, the hymnal looks to the relatively distant past; more than half the main section comes from before 1800. Watts (eight) and Wesley (nine) lead the way from the eighteenth century (total thirty-five); the nineteenth has a mere seventeen (Neale, four translations). Samples of 'recent' writing comprise W.H. Auden, Percy Dearmer, T.S. Eliot, and Andrew Young; neither the prophetic cutting edge nor the popular church favourites. The Christmas section is harder to date precisely. Two texts are by a woman: Christina Rossetti. But the book also features the Shaker song "Tis the gift to be simple', popularised by Sydney Carter in 'Lord of the dance' (1963).

A Preface by David Holbrook (Literary Editor) explains the selections, the aim being academic and educational, prompted by the desire to raise the standard of what was sung at school. The nineteenth century seems to be summed up as 'dross'; there is no Baker, Bonar, Conder, Cox, Dearmer, Dix, Ellerton, Elliott, Faber, Havergal, How, Monsell, Montgomery, Whittier or Winkworth; no kind of Williams and (of course) no Mrs Alexander. The omissions are even-handed; merit, we are told, was the sole criterion for inclusion.

The three-page 'Note' by Music Editor Elizabeth Poston commends diversity, intelligence, freedom and aspiration; together with enjoyment without stooping to mere entertainment. Some 'priceless treasures have been restored to use'; living composers were clearly told what was expected.

To make a fine distinction, here is no rubbish but plenty of nonsense, notably at Christmas.[116] As for brevity, some items are very short indeed.   In the decade before the book appeared, exciting things were stirring in Dunblane, Plymouth, Sevenoaks, even London; but there is nothing here to encourage living writers to imagine that their verses had a future.   The desire for 'fewer' hymns seems to be amply met – and even better served by another Cambridge product noticed later.

Sixteen Writers of Modest Output

Some writers have been content with one or two hymns, or struck a chord with a single text without having others which proved as effective.

Martin Franzmann (1907–1976):   An ordained Minnesota Lutheran, his life closed at Cambridge teaching theology at Westfield House. 'In Adam we have all been one' appeared in the 1969 American Lutheran *Worship Supplement*;[117] from the 1977 HSGBI Act of Praise it was taken up by UK hymnals.   Educated at Wisconsin Seminary, he taught at Northwestern College and St Louis, serving on Bible translation, doctrinal and unity commissions, and editing the New Testament volume of the *Concordia Bible with Notes*[118] (1971).

Rupert E. Davies (1909–1994):   As for others, Wesley House is the main Cambridge connection.   He studied at Oxford and Tübingen, completing his ministerial training here before working in and near Bristol, for six years as Principal of Wesley College.   He was President of the Methodist Conference, 1970–1971.   His five contributions to *H&P* are stanzas added or emended towards inclusive or more appropriate language.

---

[116] See Giles, Gordon, "Cambridge Carols" for more on *The Cambridge Hymnal*.
[117] Commission on Worship of The Lutheran Curch – Missouri Synod and Synod of Evangelical Lutheran Churches, *Worship Supplement*, Concordia Publishing House, St Louis, MO, 1969
[118] *Concordia Bible with Notes: New Testament RSV,* Concordia Publishing House, St Louis, MO, 1971

Rosemary Guillebaud (1915–2002):   From a family with a record of mission education in Central Africa spanning four generations, this Modern Languages Cambridge graduate taught for thirty years in Burundi, including Bible translation.   From 1979 she enjoyed active retirement back in the city, until her death in the nearby Addenbrooke's Hospital.   Her place here is due to a translation of a text by pastor Emmanuel Sibomana which (when supplied by Fred Barff's tune GRACE OF GOD) flourished in Grace Baptist and associated churches from the 1980's, as 'O how the grace of God amazes me'.   It appears in a supplement to *Grace Hymns*,[119] later editions of *Christian Hymns*[120] and *Praise!*   Rosemary's father Harold compiled the first bilingual hymn book for the African churches where he worked.

Maurice A.P. Wood (1916–2007):   This Queens' College and Ridley Hall man, best known as incumbent (Oxford and Islington, North London), College Principal (Oak Hill), Bishop (Norwich), booklet author and genial evangelist, also wrote 'Worship, glory, praise and honour' (published in the *Anglican Hymn Book*), a text to stand alongside 'We love the place, O God', for a 'Dedication Festival or Anniversary'.

R.J.B. (John) Eddison (1916–2011):   A graduate of Trinity (in History) and Ridley Hall, he worked with Scripture Union, 1942–1980, speaking regularly in schools, camps and youth houseparties.   The author of several books of basic doctrine, biography and practical service, from the 1940's he also wrote hymn texts. Seven appeared in *Songs of Worship* (1980), two featuring more widely: 'At the cross of Jesus I would take my place' and 'Father, although I cannot see the future you have planned'. One obituary spoke of the clarity and simplicity of their language, from 'a mind and heart steeped in the Scriptures'.

David H.G. Head (b.1922):   His Cambridge connection was Wesley House, where in 1951 he trained for ministry; among later posts was that of Superintendent of the Birmingham Mission.   His unusual baptismal hymn 'Lord, here is one to be baptized' was published in

---

[119] *Grace Hymns*, Evangelical Press / Grace Publications Trust, Orpington, Kent, 1977
[120] *Christian Hymns*, Evangelical Movement of Wales, Bridgend, 2004

Hymns and Songs; *H&P* included a form much altered by Richard Jones. From 1979 to 1986 he worked in adult education in London, also compiling collections of short, challenging prayers.

W. Hubert Vanstone (1923–1999): Though with a remarkable pastoral ministry and other writings to his credit, he became known as the author of *Love's Endeavour, Love's Expense*[121] and of the hymn, 'Morning glory, starlit sky', which forms its epilogue. Different versions are in print; it first appeared with music in *More Hymns for Today*. A graduate of both Oxford and Cambridge (St John's), the author trained for ministry at Westcott House and at Union Theological Seminary, New York; he retired in 1991 after service in the Manchester and Chester dioceses.

Anthony Coombe (b.1931): After graduating in Mathematics from Emmanuel, he trained for Anglican ministry at Tyndale Hall, Bristol, serving in Manchester, Sussex, south London and Cambridgeshire villages north-west of the city, before retiring in 1996. His one published hymn (words and music) is 'Jesus, be first in everything' (*Praise!*).

Graham S. Harrison (1935–2013): One of many with both Cambridge (Trinity Hall) and Oxford (Regent's Park) qualifications, his single pastoral ministry was at Emmanuel Evangelical Church, Newport, South Wales, 1962–2010. 'First and foremost', said an obituary, he was 'a powerful preacher and faithful pastor'. Not far behind came teaching, hymn writing and co-editing *Christian Hymns*[122] (1977 and 2004). His metrical paraphrases such as 'Unto the Lord come, raise together' (Psalm 118), translations from the Welsh and original texts, use traditional language. His widow Eluned is also a published hymn writer.

Keith Clements (b.1943): Born in West China, here is another 'Oxbridge' author; graduating at King's, he trained for Baptist ministry at Regent's Park, Oxford. He has pastored and taught in Bristol and Edinburgh, held ecumenical posts in Britain and Europe, and written on Bonhoeffer, Schleiermacher and J.H. Oldham. He

---

[121] Vanstone, W.H., *Love's Endeavour, Love's Expense*, Darton, Longman & Todd, London, 1977
[122] *Christian Hymns*, Evangelical Movement of Wales, Bridgend, 1977 and 2004

76

served on the editorial committee for *Baptist Praise and Worship*;[123] and contributed to Fred Pratt Green's Bonhoeffer paraphrase, 'By gracious powers so wonderfully sheltered.'

A. Malcolm Guite (b.1957): The author of the sonnet sequence *Sounding the Seasons*[124] has had some of his poems set to music as songs and hymns, by composers including the Canadian Steve Bell and the American J.A.C. Redford. He added a Durham PhD to studies at Pembroke College and Ridley Hall; following pastoral and teaching ministries in the Cambridge area he became Chaplain of Girton in 2003.

Christopher Hayward (1968–2007): His death at barely forty in a road accident was a severe loss to Christian music and education. His wife Helen, another singer / musician, was critically injured, but after a year resumed a near-normal life. They met while students at Corpus Christi and Peterhouse respectively; then serving at 'The Round Church', later St Andrew the Great. Qualified in theology and music, Chris taught at Oak Hill College, North London, while attached to a local congregation; further moves took in Blackburn (Lancashire) and Penshurst (Kent). An inspirational conductor and choir-leader, Chris wrote some texts and many tunes; Christopher Idle was one of those to whom he turned for new words at short notice, for which he would compose a tune, teach the choir, and introduce it the following Sunday. Many arrangements and some original items are in *Mission Praise*, *Sing Glory*, *Praise!* and annual 'Spring Harvest' collections.[125]

Richard Simpkin (b.1969): The writer of a column 'The Music Exchange' in the monthly *Evangelicals Now* (2003 to the present) is another words-and-music man whose journey has taken him from being organ scholar at Gonville and Caius, via Limehouse, East London (Pastoral Assistant) and from 1995 to St Helen's Bishopsgate in the City of London (Music Director). From its

---

[123] *Baptist Praise and Worship*, Psalms and Hymns Trust / Oxford University Press, Oxford, 1991
[124] Guite, Malcolm, *Sounding the Seasons: Seventy Sonnets for the Christian Year*, Canterbury Press, Norwich, 2012
[125] Spring Harvest Praise, Spring Harvest / Elevation, Uckfield, East Sussex, various editions since at least the mid-1980's

student and business congregation Richard drew together a group of singers and musicians for regular services and special events. He does much to encourage younger writers; his own work including 'We praise the God in whom we trust' features in local recordings, in *Praise!* and elsewhere.

Ally (Alexandra) M Barrett (b.1975): With degrees in music and theology at Clare, she worked with Jeremy Begbie ('Theology through the Arts') before training for ordination at Westcott House. Serving parishes in Godmanchester and (from 2007) Buckden, in Cambridgeshire, she is due to return in 2015 after her husband's USA sabbatical. Her most popular hymn, featuring in *Sing Praise*, the 2013 *A&M* and elsewhere, is 'Hope of our calling', written in 2006 for the Ely Diocesan Clergy Conference. Others, many set to familiar tunes, have been sung at several local events.

Phil Heaps (b.1975): This Yorkshireman graduated in Mathematics at Fitzwilliam before a career in software engineering. He wrote the first of a dozen Scripture-based hymns while a student: 'How humble Moses was' was published first in *Praise!*, and a hymn written for his wedding has been sung at several others. He is now a full-time church leader at Grace Church, Yate, near Bristol.

Craig Hudson (b.1983): Maths and music were his degree subjects at St John's; he then worked at All Souls' Langham Place, London, and (from 2012) St John's, Tunbridge Wells, Kent. His handful of songs so far have been Scripture-based, often for a younger generation.

Nineteen Writers of Medium Range

Authors with several published hymn texts include:

John R. Peacey (1896–1971): Although five hymns featured in *100 Hymns for Today* (all retained in *Common Praise*), it was not until twenty years after his death that his texts appeared in a single collection, *Go forth for God*,[126] the title being the first line of his best-known. The youngest of a bishop's ten children, he grew up in

---

[126] Hope, USA, 1991

Sussex, became a fine athlete and county cricketer, and graduated (Theology, first class) at Selwyn prior to ordination. Later he returned there as Chaplain and Dean, served in India, 1927–1945, and completed his active ministry in Bristol. In retirement, stirred by TV competitions, he began writing hymns. Another popular text is 'Awake, awake, fling off the night'; some are better-known in the USA.

Howard C.A. Gaunt (1902–1983): No relation of hymn writer Alan Gaunt, he was another sportsman who graduated from King's in 1925, taught in three public schools, but was not ordained until 1954, for ministry based at Winchester College and Cathedral. Like Canon Peacey he made his mark in *100 Hymns for Today*, which featured six texts including 'Lord Jesus, once you spoke to men'; a further three came in *More Hymns for Today*. Most are liturgical in character; *Common Praise* has five. Methodist and Baptist books have also welcomed his work.

Geoffrey Beaumont (1903–1970): Although his setting of Psalm 150 for cantor and congregation is widely published, and his *Twentieth-Century Folk Mass*[127] came in 1954, the best-known item from his pen is the tune GRACIAS from that service, for 'Now thank we all our God' as a lively alternative to NUN DANKET, reaching *The Baptist Hymn Book* in 1962. The Twentieth-Century Church Light Music Group, which he co-founded, sharply divided church and secular opinion, opening new possibilities in music and words (in that order) some years before the so-called 'hymn explosion'. Stirrings were felt in Cambridge where he studied at Trinity College; after ordination training at Ely he served as a wartime naval chaplain before returning to Trinity as Chaplain. A spell in Madrid was followed by a brief ministry at St George's, Camberwell, South London, and Warden of its Trinity College Mission; the group's publications prompted others towards similar experiments. In 1961 he joined the Community of the Resurrection at Mirfield, Yorkshire; but not before he had enthused colleagues such as Patrick Appleford, Michael Hewlett and Michael Lehr with his vision.

---

[127] Beaumont, Gerard Geoffrey Phillips, *A 20th Century Folk Mass for one or more cantors and congregations*, Josef Weinberger, London, 1960

Donald W. Hughes (1911–1967):   In the form of Emmanuel College where he studied and The Leys School where he taught, Cambridge featured strongly in his life. A headmaster in Colwyn Bay, North Wales, he had many hymn texts in manuscript, but died aged fifty-six in a road accident. With its salutary message for today, 'Creator of the earth and skies' is valued across many traditions; like other texts it was published posthumously in 1969. Some language has since been modernised or adapted.

George B. Caird (1917–1984): The URC and its part-predecessor the Congregational Union may have a higher proportion of quality hymn writers among its recent preachers than any other church grouping. One was this biblical scholar and Professor whose hymn 'Not far beyond the sea, nor high', and translations such as 'Shepherds came, their praises bringing', have travelled well beyond the circles where they originated – like his commentaries on *Luke*[128] and *Revelation*.[129] Though his academic career at Oxford (Mansfield College, student and Principal) outweighs his Cambridge years, his first degree was at Peterhouse. He was Moderator of the URC's General Assembly 1975–1976, and an observer at the Second Vatican Council. Social and global concerns were evident in his Christian pacifism; as a member of the Fellowship of Reconciliation, he consistently commended its non-violent theology of justice and peace.

Patrick R.N. Appleford (b.1925):   A pioneer in the Twentieth-Century Church Light Music Group and its first secretary, he became best-known for his 1958 hymn 'Lord Jesus Christ, you have come to us' to his cheerful tune LIVING LORD. Originally a Communion hymn, it was written when he was a curate in Poplar, East London, published in 1960, and soon appeared widely. The tune has also been set to James Seddon's 'To him we come' (1964). The author graduated from Trinity College and trained for ordination at Chichester (Hampshire); he served as a college chaplain and as Dean of Lusaka, Zambia, later working in Chelmsford, Essex, as Diocesan Director of Education, 1975-90.

---

[128] Caird, G.B., *The Gospel of St.Luke (Pelican Gospel Commentary)*, Penguin Books, London, 1971

Caird, G.B., *The Revelation of St.John the Divine* (Black's New Testament Commentaries), A. & C. Black Ltd., London, 1966

Richard G. Jones (b.1926): A graduate of St John's, he trained for Methodist ministry at Hartley Victoria College, Manchester, later returning as Tutor, then Principal. Most of his early service was in northern England, but latterly he became East Anglia's District Chairman before moving to Nottingham. He chaired the main committee for *H&P*, to which he contributed 'Come, all who look to Christ today' and one revision. He has also had a major role in Methodist–Roman Catholic conversations.

Basil E. Bridge (b.1927):   Another in a strong team of Congregational / URC hymn writers, he trained at Cheshunt College, Cambridge and served churches in Warwickshire, Leicester, Lincolnshire and Bedford, retiring to his home city, Norwich. A long-term active member of HSGBI, he wrote 'The Son of God proclaim' in 1962, and twenty-four years later (after widespread publication) used its first line as the title for his own collection.[130] His wedding hymn 'Jesus, Lord, we pray' features in many books; three hymns (not the same three) are in each of *HTC*, *R&S*, and *Common Praise*, whereas both *New Start*[131] and the 2013 *A&M* have five.

Doreen (Bunty) Newport (1927–2004): Her first published hymn was 'Think of a world without any flowers', printed in the seminal *Dunblane Praises 2*[132] in 1967, and in many collections since. Its opening line has proved memorable enough to be varied, adapted, even parodied. It emerged from a junior class at Emmanuel Congregational Church, Cambridge, 'half-invented by the children', until Peter Cutts formalised its arrangement. Although *R&S* includes her music to Judith O'Neill's similarly lyrical 'Song of praise for all the saints', the composer should not be typecast as 'merely' a children's writer. Having studied French and Music at Oxford, trained as a teacher in Manchester and taught in Norfolk, she moved to Cambridge with husband Jack, President of Cheshunt College (later joint-Principal of Cheshunt and Westminster Colleges). Latterly she taught music at Winchester where in 1993 she conducted the HSGBI Act of Praise.

Bridge, Basil, *The Son Of God Proclaim And Other Hymns*, United Reformed Church, 1986
New Start Hymns and Songs, Kevin Mayhew, Stowmarket, Suffolk, 1999
Dunblane Praises 2, Scottish Churches' Music Consultation, Dunblane, 1967

Alan H.F. Luff (b.1928):   Few Cambridge alumni have done as much for hymnody as this Cathedral Canon. Now retired to Cardiff, South Wales, he came from Oxford to train for ordination at Westcott House. He then served in Wales and England, and held cathedral posts in Manchester, London (Westminster Abbey) and Birmingham. A Welsh speaker in adulthood, in 1990 he wrote *Welsh Hymns and their Tunes*[133]; he contributed *A Hymn Book Survey 1993–2003* to the HSGBI's second series of Occasional Papers, and in 2005 edited *Strengthen for Service: 100 years of The English Hymnal.*[134] He has often addressed HSGBI conferences – once almost impromptu, replacing a visiting speaker who failed to appear. Many years on the Society's committee have included roles as Secretary, Chairman and Bulletin contributor; he is currently one of three Honorary Vice-Presidents. He has shared actively in all the sister societies, where his language skills are invaluable. He has written chapters in symposia to honour Harry Eskew [135] and Donald Hustad. [136]   At Westminster Abbey he organised an annual 'Come and Sing' lunchtime series introducing many new hymns and hymnals. Several texts and tunes include 'Year by year, from past to future' (*Sing Praise*) and words to mark the inauguration of the first Welsh Assembly. He was on the main committee for *H&P*, which includes four of his Scripture-based texts.

Ann Phillips (b.1930): Best-known among hymn lovers for her text on the Holy Spirit in creation ('Into a world of dark',) this Oxford graduate came to Cambridge, first as Chief Sub-editor for the University Press, then as Librarian and Tutor of Newnham. That hymn was introduced at Emmanuel URC where she was an Elder, in 1972; three years later it was published, slightly altered, in *New Church Praise*. She has written for children, edited school poetry

---

Luff, Alan, *Welsh Hymns and Their Tunes: Their Background and Place in Welsh History and Culture*, Stainer & Bell, London and Hope Publishing, Carol Stream, IL, 1990

Luff, Alan (Ed.), *Strengthen for Service: 100 years of The English Hymnal,* Canterbury Press, Norwich, 2005

Powell, Paul R. (Ed.), *Hymnology in the Service of the Church: Essays in Honor of Harry Eskew,* Morning Star Music Publishers, St Louis, MO, 2008

Richardson, Paul A., and Sharp, Timothy W. (Eds.), *Jubilate, Amen!: A Festschrift in Honor of Donald Paul Hustad*, Pendragon Press, Hillsdale, NY, 2009

textbooks, specialised in seventeenth-century English verse, and served on the committees for *H&P* and *R&S*.

Ivor H. Jones (b.1934): A Methodist Yorkshireman whose education took in Sheffield, Oxford (organ scholar, Brasenose), Bristol (PhD) and Heidelberg, he chose Wesley House for his ministerial training, later returning as Principal. He served several circuits while continuing to teach and write, including New Testament studies; as secretary he helped to produce the supplement *Hymns and Songs* (1969), and as convenor its major successor *H&P*. Both books include 'Christ our King before creation', written to meet a minor publishing crisis and subsequently revised to be gender-inclusive. *H&P*, subtitled 'a Methodist and Ecumenical Hymn Book', was envisaged originally as a joint production with the URC; this plan was later modified, and its eventual Preface, signed jointly by two Joneses, Richard G. and Ivor H., refers back to the 1933 *Methodist Hymn Book*[137] and to John Wesley's 1779 *Preface* as benchmarks. It specially commends the Psalm versions, and a book 'which makes available to all Christians the riches of classical, evangelical, catholic and charismatic hymnody of the past and present'.

Richard T. Bewes (b.1934): After ministries in Essex, Middlesex, and twenty years at All Souls' Langham Place in London's West End, since formal retirement in 2004 he continues to span continents, notably Africa (he was born in Kenya to missionary parents) and North America. Cambridge for him meant Emmanuel and Ridley Hall. An author of many paperbacks, he began writing hymns and songs in the 1960s, co-editing *Youth Praise 1* and *2*, followed by *Psalm Praise* and *HTC*. Most popular is a Psalm 46 paraphrase set to the DAM BUSTERS film tune, 'God is our strength and refuge'. Among colleagues have been Michael Perry and musicians Christian Strover, David Iliff, John Barnard and Noël Tredinnick. With the last-named as conductor he has hosted many 'Prom Praise' events at London's Royal Albert Hall. He has worked closely with Bishop Festo Kivengere in Kenya and Dr Billy Graham in the USA, combining teaching, preaching and Bible-based video with a long-term zeal for tennis and sport-related ministry.

---

[137] *Methodist Hymn Book*, Methodist Publishing House, Peterborough, 1933

Norman L. Warren (b.1934): One of the most prolific composers in the Jubilate group, he read Music and Modern Languages at Corpus Christi before proceeding to Ridley Hall. Following parish ministry in Warwickshire and Surrey he became Archdeacon of Rochester, Kent, retiring in 2000. He contributed to *Youth Praise*, *Psalm Praise* (forty-nine tunes and many Psalm chants), *HTC* and other books, with a major hand in *Church Family Worship*[138] and *Carol Praise*. He has composed some two hundred tunes and some texts; his illustrated evangelistic booklet *Journey Into Life*[139] has worldwide sales exceeding forty million.

Stephen Orchard (b.1942): After preparing for the Congregational ministry, later the URC, at Trinity College, he pastored churches in Caerphilly (South Wales), Sutton (Surrey) and Welwyn (Hertfordshire), serving in ecumenical posts and as Director of the Christian Education Movement before returning to Cambridge in 2000 as Principal of Westminster College. His hymn texts appear in *R&S*, *Praise!* and the 2013 *A&M*, and include a fresh translation of Martin Luther's 'Ein' feste Burg': 'Our God stands like a fortress rock.' He retired in 2007.

Hilary Jolly (b.1945): Living in the city for many years, she has worked for St Andrew the Great church (formerly at the historic 'Round Church') and St Philip's, and for charitable organisations in Cambridge. As the winner of the St Paul's Cathedral Millennium Hymn Competition with 'Through the darkness of the ages' she surprised many because the seven hundred entries included some well-established authors, while she was little-known beyond Cambridge. Texts were assessed anonymously and, once paired with the winning tune by Paul Bryan, her words were sung at major events celebrating the dawn of AD2000. For her, COE FEN is not primarily the name of Kenneth Naylor's acclaimed tune, but of green pastures on the southern side of Cambridge, where she would often mentally craft a hymn while walking her dog. Some early writing was encouraged by Christopher Hayward; more appears in *Praise!* and on the Jubilate website. Some forty of her collected hymns are due to be published soon.

---

[138] Perry, Michael (Ed.), *Church Family Worship*, Hodder & Stoughton, London, 1986
[139] Warren, Norman, *Journey Into Life*, Falcon Booklets, London, 1963

Sue Gilmurray (b.1950): 'I seem to inhabit the borderline between hymn and song', writes this singer / musician who as a schoolgirl had a song published in *Faith, Folk and Clarity*.[140] She has written, composed, played and sung many more, from carol, folk and protest items to texts in traditional hymn mode. With an Oxford Classics degree and qualifications in Education and Information Studies, she has worked in London's Church House Bookshop, and from 1987 to 2013 in the Cambridgeshire College of Arts and Technology, later Anglia Ruskin University, latterly as Music and Arts Librarian. In 1994 she joined the Anglican Pacifist Fellowship, for which she has recorded CD's including secular material[141] for the Movement for the Abolition of War. A keyboard player and chorister at St Mary's, Ely and a regular at the 'Greenbelt' Christian arts festival, in 2014 she shared a joint session with Chris Idle on 'Hymns and songs of peace and war' at the HSGBI conference held near her birthplace in Cirencester, Gloucestershire. Her published work appears in the periodical *Worship Live*,[142] *Hunger for Justice*[143] and *Songs for the Road to Peace*.[144] 'The war machine rolls round' is 'the one that has travelled furthest'.

Maggi Dawn (b.1959): Her name became widely known from around 1990, when her scripture-based song 'He was bruised for our transgressions' appeared in *Mission Praise* and elsewhere. She has rich associations with Cambridge, first studying at Fitzwilliam College and Ridley Hall. After a curacy at nearby Ely she returned to Cambridge as Chaplain at King's and then at

---

[140] Smith, Peter (Ed.), *Faith, Folk and Clarity: A Collection of Folk Songs*, Galliard, London, 1967
[141] CD *The Way of Peace*, 2001
[142] http://www.worshiplive.org.uk/, accessed 25/01/2015
[143] Nicholls, Martin John (Ed.), *Hunger for Justice: Hymns and Songs to Change the World*, Christian Aid / Kevin Mayhew Ltd, Stowmarket, 2004
[144] Idle, Christopher and Gilmurray, Sue, *Songs for the Road to Peace*, Anglican Pacifist Fellowship, Milton Keynes, 2008. A CD of the same name is also available.

Robinson College, venue for the 2015 conference of three hymn societies. She often contributes to the annual 'Greenbelt' festival, writes widely on liturgy, and completed a PhD on Samuel Taylor Coleridge at Selwyn. She identifies with a 'post-evangelical' commitment to the emerging church. She is currently Associate Dean and Professor at Yale University in the USA.

Daniel Chua (b.1966): Currently Professor of Music at the University of Hong Kong, his previous work includes a BA (Music, first class) from St Catharine's followed by PhD and M Phil at St John's where he became Director of Studies in Music, and Research Fellow. Senior posts at King's, London, preceded his move to Hong Kong in 2008. His writing includes work on Beethoven, Monteverdi and Stravinsky, and among several published hymns the most widely sung is 'Jesus is Lord! Behold the King of kings', featured in British, American and Asian books.

Three Marathon Men

A trio of Cambridge authors have over 100 published hymns each.

✓ **Timothy Dudley-Smith** (b.1926): One of the pioneering hymn writers of the late twentieth century and early twenty-first, 'TDS', born in Manchester and growing up in Derbyshire and Kent, is a classic example of Cambridge style. Graduating from Pembroke, he went on to study at Ridley Hall; the connection was maintained by leadership and chaplaincy of the Cambridge University Mission in Bermondsey, SE London (now the Salmon Centre). He became Archdeacon of Norwich, then Bishop of Thetford, Norfolk, from 1981 to his retirement near Salisbury, Wiltshire, in 1992. His hymn-writing began unexpectedly; he paraphrased the Magnificat (NEB version) with no thought of producing a hymn; 'Tell out, my soul, the greatness of the Lord' became a fixture in most hymnals since the *Anglican Hymn Book* – but only when set to WOODLANDS in 1969. Since then over four hundred texts have been published; his Christmas card features a new one annually, while 'Lord, for the years' crosses many denominational boundaries. While the hymns deal with global, national, social and personal issues, the evangelical note is ever-present; Christ's atoning death, historic resurrection and eternal gospel are never far from the author's mind and heart. In 2007 he was awarded the OBE for services to hymnody and in 2009 an Hon. DD from Durham. He is a Life Member and Fellow of the North American Hymn Society and an Honorary Vice-President of HSGBI. His editorial work spans *Psalm Praise* and *Common Praise*; among several collections of his texts, the fullest recent book is a second volume of *A House of Praise*.[145]

David Mowbray (b.1938): If it was a conference at St George's, Windsor in 1978 which first prompted him to try his hand at hymn-writing, Fitzwilliam House (later, College) in Cambridge and his English degree set him on track for the ministry which interacted with his writing. After ordination training in Bristol, he served parishes in three counties, retiring to Lincoln in 2004. He issued three home-produced collections, mainly for traditional tunes; *Partners in Praise*[146] published two texts including a rare one on the sheep and the goats (Matthew 7). Sixteen featured in *HTC*, soon after which he joined the Jubilate group for further writing and editing. He often contributed texts for the periodical *Hymns and Congregational Songs*.[147] Most popular has been 'Come to us, creative Spirit'; he has also written about Sunday ('First of the week and finest day'), scriptural and other 'saints and personalities', mental heath, hospices, and the environment. His own collection, *Sing, God's Easter People*,[148] appeared in 2012.

Michael A. Perry (1942–1996): The Cambridge connection was brief, part of his ordination training being at Ridley Hall. But his contribution to hymnody from the late 1960s was

---

[145] Dudley-Smith, Timothy, *A House of Praise: Collected Hymns 1961-2001*, Oxford University Press, Oxford, 2003; second volume, 2015
[146] Braley, Bernard and Pratt Green, Fred Pratt (Eds.), *Partners in Praise*, Stainer & Bell, London, 1979
[147] Braley, Bernard and Luff, Alan (Eds.), *Hymns and Congregational Songs*, Stainer & Bell, London, c.1988
[148] Mowbray, David, *Sing, God's Easter People: Hymns, Carols, Worship Songs*, published by the author, 2012

huge. One of five Cambridge men in the editorial team for *Psalm Praise*, he then played a major writing and editing part in *HTC*. Many other collections followed, most under the 'Jubilate' imprint and flowing from his initiatives while an Anglican incumbent in Bitterne (Southampton), Eversley (Hampshire) and Tonbridge (Kent). A year before his death at fifty-four from a brain tumour, his hymn texts were collected in *Singing to God*,[149] from lighter pieces for children to substantial hymns in classic style. His handbook *Preparing for Worship*,[150] where he distances himself from the 'Adam lay ybounden' school of carol-singing, dates from that time. Among his hymns are 'O God beyond all praising' and 'Bring to the Lord a glad new song', set to well-known music by Holst and Parry. An occasional composer himself, he visited North America and West Africa in the cause of hymns, and did much to encourage younger writers.

More Hymnologists, Editors and Composers

This diverse group varies between those for whom hymns are or were a lifelong commitment, and others devoted mainly to a single project.

John Dykes Bower (1905–1981): Organ scholar at Corpus Christi, he held posts at Truro, Oxford, Durham, and London's St Paul's Cathedral. He was joint Music Editor of *A&M Revised* (1950), a standard book for three decades which did not reveal the editors' names and was the last edition with indexes at the front. He also co-edited *100 Hymns for Today* and *More Hymns for Today*, which merged with the next major edition. Four tunes are in the 2013 book; he was knighted in 1968.

---

[149] Perry, Michael, *Singing to God: Hymns and Songs 1965-1995*, Hope Publishing Company, Carol Stream, IL, 1995
[150] Perry, Michael, *Preparing for Worship*, Marshall Pickering, London, 1995

Elizabeth Poston (1905–1987): Her role as Music Editor of *The Cambridge Hymnal* is sketched above; a composer, pianist and author, she trained at the RAM, graduating in 1925 before travelling abroad, studying architecture and collecting folksongs. In 1939 she joined the BBC's European Service as its wartime Director of Music, afterwards helping to establish the Third Programme (subsequently Radio 3). She composed music for radio and television; among collaborators were C.S. Lewis, Dylan Thomas, Ralph Vaughan Williams and 'Peter Warlock', whose work she presented in a five-part broadcast series. She was President of the Society of Women Musicians and wrote for the Arts Council of Great Britain; several of her songs are published. Among tunes, arrangements and descants in *The Cambridge Hymnal*, her music for the eighteenth-century carol 'Jesus Christ the apple tree' has become most popular.

John Whitridge Wilson (1905–1992): This 'bear of a man' (as a friend called him), not to be confused with his North American namesake, was a lovable creature of occasional fierceness but great brain and an unrivalled knowledge of hymn tunes. A Cambridge graduate in Physics and Mathematics, he made music his career; after study at RCM he taught at Charterhouse School in Surrey, 1932-64, with a wartime interlude of classroom science. For fifteen more years he taught at RCM, which published many of his hymn and anthem tunes. A wide range of jointly-edited books spanned the 1936 *Clarendon Hymn Book* [151] to *H&P*. He contributed massively to the HSGBI as treasurer, writer and speaker, illustrating each point from the piano. He masterminded the Annual Act of Praise (Festival of Hymns), addressed the North American Society, and worked with Erik Routley and Fred Pratt Green. His friendship with the latter, prompting many themes and texts, extended FPG's role from published poet to Methodism's leading hymn writer.

Herbert C. Taylor (1906–1996): Vicar of Christ Church, Orpington, Kent (where he founded the youth movement Pathfinders) from 1942 until his retirement to Tonbridge in 1973, his choir included future hymn writers Michael Baughen and Michael Saward. A

---

[151] *Clarendon Hymn Book, Oxford University Press, Oxford, 1936*

graduate of Emmanuel and Ridley Hall, he chaired the committee for the *Anglican Hymn Book*, then a landmark hymnal for evangelical Anglicans. He briefly led a group planning its successor, which ultimately found no publisher.

Gerald H. Knight (1908–1979): A Cornishman who at fourteen became Assistant Organist at Truro Cathedral, he went on to Peterhouse as organ scholar. Studies at RCM and posts in London and at Canterbury Cathedral prepared him for twenty years as RSCM's Director, and five more as its Overseas Commissioner. He was joint Music Editor of the 1950 *A&M Revised* and also worked on both supplements.

Norman P. Goldhawk (1909–2001): Another in a distinguished line of HSGBI Chairmen / Presidents who held that office 1980-83, having belonged since 1937; after reading Modern Languages in London, he trained for Methodist ministry at Wesley House. Pastoral posts in Scotland and England were followed by twenty years teaching at Richmond Theological College, Surrey. He chaired the committee for *Hymns and Songs* (1969) and, said Dr Bernard Massey, 'wrote its elegant Preface' – anonymously. He was a local church organist, active in the Methodist Church Music Society; among his varied writings were translations of German theology, chapters on Methodist history, and in 1979 *On Hymns and Hymn-books*[152], described by Professor J.R. Watson as 'too modest ... one of the first to engage with a new generation of hymnwriters.' Later he became a significant contributor to the *Companion to Hymns and Psalms.*[153]

Mervyn Horder (1910–1997): The word 'eccentric' might have been coined to describe the second and last Lord Horder. The son (and biographer) of the King's physician Sir Thomas Horder, and therefore an hereditary peer, he never entered the House of Lords, but after Winchester and Trinity College became chairman of Duckworths (publishers), 1948–1970, while living simply in his cluttered North London mews flat. Active in the HSGBI, he

---

[152] Epworth Press
[153] Trickett, Kenneth and Watson, J.R. (Eds.), *Companion to Hymns and Psalms,* Methodist Publishing House, Peterborough, 1988

compiled *The Easter Carol Book*,[154] contributed to several periodicals, and wrote texts and many tunes, three appearing in *Praise!* He set to music words by Shakespeare, Burns, Dorothy Parker and John Betjeman, and into his eighties cycled regularly to church choir practice.

F. Derek Kidner (1913–2008): Gifted in words and music, he is known to many through his pithy Bible commentaries, including those on Genesis, Proverbs and supremely on the Psalms,[155] much reprinted. Two spells at Cambridge comprised student years at Christ's and Ridley Hall (double first, Economics and Theology) and as Warden of Tyndale House research centre until retirement to Histon, north of Cambridge. He served on the editorial team for *Christian Praise*[156] and the *Anglican Hymn Book*, and became a valued mentor and friend to Timothy Dudley-Smith.

Ronald E.C. Johnson (1913–1996): Born and educated in Portsmouth, Hampshire, this Englishman was awarded the hard-earned title of 'Honorary Scot'. Graduating from St John's, he joined the Civil Service and in 1935 was summoned to the Scottish Office in Edinburgh, where he made his home. Dramatic wartime naval exploits were followed by work in the Scottish Home and Health Department, as Secretary from 1963, then Secretary for Commissions, 1972–1978, a key policy adviser to successive British governments. Known as a hard and fast worker and elegant writer, and described in the Scottish press as a 'kenspeckle' (conspicuous) figure, he was awarded the CBE in 1962 and knighted in 1970. He was choirmaster and President of the Edinburgh Bach Society and for thirty years organist at St Columba's Episcopal Church. Half way through one government committee he excused himself in order 'to go and tune a virginal'. He was a leading member of the HSGBI for most of its first fifty years.

Henry Chadwick (1920–2008): To say that he chaired the editorial committee for *Common Praise*, the 2000 edition in the long *A&M*

---

[154] Schott Music, 1982
[155] Kidner, Derek, *Tyndale Old Testament Commentaries*, Inter-Varsity Press, Leicester: *Genesis*, 1967; *Proverbs*, 1964; *Psalms*, 1973 (Books I and II) and 1975 (Books III to V)
[156] *Christian Praise*, Tyndale Press, Bristol, 1957

series, would be to choose one detail from a glittering career of academic and literary achievement. One of a family of distinguished Chadwicks, his Cambridge years began as a student at Magdalene and Ridley Hall. He became Chaplain and then Dean of Queens', and in addition to other doctorates he was Regius Professor of Divinity and Master of Peterhouse. As one of the *A&M* proprietors he also co-edited *100 Hymns for Today* and *More Hymns for Today*, both incorporated into *A&M New Standard* (1983). His engaging biography of Augustine of Hippo[157] was published posthumously in 2009.

David Holbrook (1923–2011): The Literary Editor of *The Cambridge Hymnal*, who expressed himself forcibly in its Introduction (see above), will always be associated with the city in that role. Like Percy Dearmer in *Songs of Praise*[158] fifty years earlier, though with different emphasis, he enlisted classic poets in the service of hymnody. Free from the constraints of a committee, he stamped his own philosophy on the book.

Anthony D. Caesar (b.1924): Mixed reviews greeted the *NEH* on its appearance in 1986. But as the first major revision of *EH* in a hundred years it enjoyed immense success, becoming the expected book in many cathedrals, and in parish churches which robustly guard their Anglo-catholic tradition and are not greatly moved by contemporary trends. Chaired by hymn-writing archdeacon George Timms, the committee included this cleric as Music Editor among its seven members; like three others he had no part in compiling the 1975 supplement *English Praise*.[159] A graduate of Magdalene, he trained for ordination at Oxford and was RSCM's Chaplain for five years. He spent five more on clergy selection boards and then as a royal chaplain, retiring in 1991 and living latterly in Cheltenham, Gloucestershire.

William B.J. Llewellyn (b.1925): After Emmanuel College and the RAM, most of his career was spent teaching at Charterhouse School in Surrey, then twelve years chairing the RSCM's Devon

---

[157] Chadwick, Henry, *Augustine of Hippo: A Life*, Oxford University Press, Oxford, 2009
[158] Oxford University Press, Oxford, 1925; revised and enlarged edition, 1931
[159] *English Praise*, Oxford University Press, Oxford, 1975

branch. In 1986 he produced *The Novello Book of Carols*;[160] he has composed tunes for Timothy Dudley-Smith's words and edited several smaller RSCM collections of his hymns.[161]

Annette Farrer (1930–2009): An Oxford graduate who studied English under C.S. Lewis and Dame Helen Gardner, she lived in Cambridge 1978-92, when her husband Michael was Vicar of St Paul's. From student days onwards she sang in the Bach Choir and other choral groups. In semi-retirement they moved to nearby Ely; she served on two hymnal committees, one chaired by Herbert Taylor, then Geoffrey Whitehead; the second resulted in *Sing Glory*.

Peter W. Cutts (b.1937): This influential figure for church music on both sides of the Atlantic went from Clare College, where he graduated, to Mansfield, Oxford. After twenty-five years teaching music in Yorkshire he moved to Massachusetts in 1989 to be Director of Music for several churches, and in retirement returned to West Yorkshire. He chaired the committee for *New Church Praise* which has thirteen of his tunes; seven are in *R&S*, while some of his hundred-and-thirty-plus feature in several North American hymnals. The best-known, BRIDEGROOM, was composed for Emma Frances? Bevan's 'As the bridegroom to his chosen', published in *100 Hymns for Today*. In 2005 he revised and enlarged Erik Routley's *An English-Speaking Hymnal Guide*.[162]

Gwilym Beechey (b.1938): As well as studying at the RCM, his years at Magdalene College (music scholar and research student, 1956-62) led to school-teaching followed by lecturing posts at the Universities of Glasgow and Hull. As a player and arranger of recorder music he edited the journal *The Consort*[163] from 1986 to 1993, and he is currently organist at his parish church in Peterborough. His compositions include hymn tunes, canticle settings, chants, introits, anthems and many organ works, and he

---

[160] Llewellyn, William (Ed.), *The Novello Book of Carols*, Novello & Co, London, 1986
A recent example is Dudley-Smith, Timothy and Llewellyn, William, *A Mirror to the Soul: 30 Contemporary hymns based on psalms*, RSCM, Salisbury, 2013
[162] Routley, Erik, *An English-Speaking Hymnal Guide*, GIA Publications, Chicago, IL, 1979; Routley, Erik, and Cutts, Peter W., *An English-Speaking Hymnal Guide, Edited and Expanded*, GIA Publications, Chicago, IL, 2005
[163] The Consort – Journal of the Dolmetsch Foundation, Haslemere, Surrey. http://www.dolmetsch.com/drupal-6.19/drupal-6.19/node, accessed 01/02/2015.

has edited and written widely about music, notably of the seventeenth and eighteenth centuries. At Cambridge he gained his PhD and several other musical qualifications.

David R. Wright (1939–2009): Graduating in Geography from St Catharine's, he taught in Hertfordshire before becoming a Lecturer at Keswick Hall, Norwich (Norfolk), which in 1981 became part of the University of East Anglia. With his wife Jill he compiled a series of innovative school atlases, notably the *Philip's Children's Atlas*.[164] They also published three succinct books on the hymns of the Wesleys and others.[165] While living in the Norfolk village of Mulbarton for thirty-five years, taking an active part in the parish church, school, local history and journalism, their shared love of travel for both pleasure and school trips took them to Italy, Morocco, Tunisia, India, Ghana and Australia. In 1976 David held a teacher fellowship in Development at the School of Oriental and African Studies, and later gained a London MA in Geography and Education. As well as expertise in railways, coins and postage stamps, he was a stimulating member of the Association of Christian Writers and the HSGBI. He contributed much to the latter in committee, conference and print, on metre, military language, and hymnals. Just before his death from cancer he completed in hospital an Occasional Paper on *What Do Hymns Say About Daily Work?* [166]– his conclusion: not enough.

David G. Wilson (b.1940): A graduate of Manchester (in Botany) as well as Clare College and Ridley Hall in Cambridge, he shared with others in editing *Youth Praise* (including his tune

---

[164] Wright, David & Jill, Philip's Children's Atlas, Philip's, London, 1987; 13th Edition, 2013
[165] Wright, David & Jill, *Praise with Understanding – an Encounter with Thirty Hymns*; *Thirty Hymns of the Wesleys*; *Thirty Christmas Hymns*, Paternoster Press, Exeter, respectively 1983, 1985 and 1989
[166] Wright, David R., *What Do Hymns Say About Daily Work?*, The Hymn Society of Great Britain and Ireland, Northwich, Cheshire, 2010

A PURPLE ROBE), *Psalm Praise* (twenty-five tunes) and *HTC* (Music Editor). Ordained in 1965, he ministered in Leicester, London and Middlesex parishes while continuing his musical and choral work. Several tunes feature in later collections and hymnals (*Songs of Worship, Carol Praise, Sing Glory, Praise!* A&M 2013 etc). He retired to Southampton in 2005.

Michael Lehr (1943–2010): During his Cambridge years he sang in Trinity College choir and played bass guitar in a rock band. An encounter with the Twentieth-Century Church Light Music Group led him to join; he led others to advance from composing tunes for classic texts into more original work, writing his own guitar-based Communion setting and other texts with tunes, published in the 1960's. Graduating in Geography, he worked for some years in town planning, while recording several songs with 'Reflection Christian Music' including some from Sydney Carter and *Psalm Praise*. For his church at Wellingborough, Northamptonshire, he wrote new hymns and arrangements of older ones, some being available on the RCM website, and joined the Christian Songwriting Organisation to help other writers. One obituary said, 'He had a real passion for helping people improve their songwriting skills.' With John Hartley he led a session at the 2007 HSGBI conference, but his remaining years were a struggle against ill-health.

John Barnard (b.1948): A Selwyn College graduate (1969), he has been active in church music as well as teaching German at his old school, John Lyon in Harrow. He served on the music committee for *HTC, Sing Glory* and the 2013 A&M, all of which include several of his tunes; and for many other collections from Jubilate and RSCM. With David Iliff he prepared the RSCM's major choir resources *The Carol Book*[167] and *Season by Season.*[168] He collaborated with the late Paul Wigmore, poet and hymn writer, at the annual Edington Festival in Wiltshire; in 2008 he wrote the HSGBI Guide to *Understanding Hymn Tunes.* [169] Among

---

[167] Iliff, David and Barnard, John (Eds.), *The Carol Book* and *The RSCM Carol Book Supplement*, RSCM, Salisbury, 2005 and 2009
[168] Barnard, John and Iliff, David (Eds.), *Season by Season: Music for Times & Seasons*, RSCM, Salisbury, 2008
[169] Barnard, John, *Understanding Hymn Tunes*, The Hymn Society of Great Britain and Ireland, Northwich, Cheshire, 2008

compositions and many arrangements is the acclaimed GUITING POWER, which in 1982 gave wider scope to Michael Saward's 'Christ triumphant'.

Paul Bryan (b.1950): A notable Cambridge success paired the words of Hilary Jolly with his tune subsequently named ST PAUL'S CATHEDRAL. These were the winners in words and music respectively of the St Paul's Cathedral Millennium hymn competition, entered separately but linked by the judges and published together. Both entries have since then also found new partners, as in *Praise!* and *Sing Praise*. For over twenty years he was Director of Music at St John's College Choir School; now a widely-travelled freelance composer, organist and pianist, he has written some hundred works for choir and organ, many of them available from Cambridge Recordings.

Angela C.W. Tilby (b.1950): It is always good to hear a broadcaster who knows what she is talking about when introducing a hymn. Here is one, who had a strong record at Cambridge and at the BBC before becoming Diocesan Canon of Christ Church, Oxford in 2011. She graduated from Girton, and was for twenty-two years a producer in the BBC's Religious Department. She studied at Durham for eventual Anglican ordination in 1997. She became Tutor, then Vice-Principal of Westcott House, from 2007 Vicar of St Benet's Church, Cambridge before moving to Oxford. A frequent contributor to 'Thought for the Day' and BBC radio's daily 'Act of Worship', she has written widely on hymns, prayer and the seven deadly sins, and regularly for the Church Times.

Rowan D. Williams (b.1950): Both before and after becoming the hundred-and-fourth Archbishop of Canterbury, leading the Anglican Communion during one of its more turbulent decades, this distinguished scholar was a speaker at HSGBI conferences; his current office of Honorary President is more than a formality which goes with Lambeth Palace. Graduating from Christ's, after further study at Oxford he went to the College of the Resurrection at Mirfield, Yorkshire. He taught at Westcott House and was Dean of Clare, then Lady Margaret Professor of Divinity at Oxford (1986–1992) before becoming Bishop of Monmouth and Archbishop of Wales, 1999–2002. These appointments interlocked with much writing, lecturing and pastoral work; among his books are volumes on poetry, politics, and theological, social, moral and international issues. In addition to English and Welsh he speaks several other languages; in 2012 he unexpectedly resigned as Archbishop to become Master of Magdalene; the following year he became a life peer as Baron Williams of Oystermouth (Swansea, South Wales) and Chancellor of the University of South Wales.

Charles M. Stewart (b.1950): Graduating from St John's, after a spell of teaching he trained for Anglican ministry at Oxford; two curacies were followed by time as Precentor at Winchester Cathedral (1994–2006), since when he has been Vicar of Walton-on-Thames, Surrey. He worked with Alan Luff and others in compiling *Sing His Glory*,[170] a guide to hymns matching the three-

---

[170] Ed. Alan Dunstan and others; Canterbury Press, 1997. The Revised and Enlarged 3rd edition (Ed. Alan Luff) dates from 2013.

year Lectionary, enlarged in 2007 as *Sing God's Glory*, covering fourteen main hymnals and some single-author collections.

[Anthony] Paul Leddington Wright (b.1951):   After making at seventeen his first North American visit as a recitalist, he became organ scholar at St Catharine's, then organist at Anglican and Methodist churches, also working with the Methodist Association of Youth Clubs.   He was Coventry Cathedral's Director of Music, 1984-95, where he founded St Michael's Singers and led their recitals and recordings.   He then spent some years with the BBC, including TV's 'Songs of Praise' hymn programme.   One of his many tunes, EMMA, features in *H&P*, where he is named as Anthony Paul Wright.   More recently he has returned to his love of musical theatre and opera.

Paul J. Ferguson (b.1955):   Like Charles Stewart, he worked on *Sing His Glory* and *Sing God's Glory*, while serving at York Minster as Precentor from 1995.   He gained his FRCO in 1975, and after degrees from Oxford (in Music) and Cambridge (King's) he studied at Westcott House.   He joined the Westminster Abbey staff (Chaplain, then Precentor) before moving to York; in 2001 he became Archdeacon of Cleveland (North Yorkshire), and from 2014, Suffragan Bishop of Whitby.

John P. Hartley (b.1956):   After studies at Cambridge (Mathematics at Corpus Christi) and the Universities of Leeds (PhD) and Durham (BA), he was ordained and ministered in London, Kent and Lichfield (Staffordshire).   He became the area 'Faith in the City' Officer, and from 2000 vicar of Eccleshill, West Yorkshire.   He has served on the Executive of the HSGBI, written hymn texts, and often contributed to its Bulletin and annual conferences.

Jeremy S. Begbie (b.1957):   Before moving to North Carolina in 2009, he collected several degrees and enjoyed a Cambridge career in theology and music.   He first graduated from Edinburgh, gaining a BD and PhD in Aberdeen; after a curacy he returned to Ridley Hall where he had trained for ordination, as Chaplain, Director of Studies, Vice-Principal and then Associate Principal.   He was a team-member for the supplement *Anglican Praise* and began to write widely on church music before moving back to Scotland for a post at St Andrew's, then in 2009 to the USA, as Research Professor at Duke University Divinity School, Durham, NC, specialising in the relationship between theology and the arts. A trained pianist, his music qualifications include ARCM and LRAM.

Gordon J. Giles (b.1966): His most recent enterprise linking Cambridge with hymns is his joint-editorship of the present booklet. He knows the city through Magdalene College, where he studied philosophy following a first degree in music at Lancaster, and Ridley Hall where he trained for Anglican ministry. After serving in Arbury (Chesterton) on the edge of the city, then at St Paul's Cathedral, he became Vicar of Enfield Chase in North London in 2003. He has written short commentaries on hymns for the RSCM journal *Church Music Quarterly*, and the HSGBI published his collection of hymn-based prayers, *Praying Thrice*.[171] He has also written several books on hymns and anthems for the BRF and SPCK (Paraclete Press in the USA). He is a Director of the English Hymnal Company and served on the committee for the 2013 *A&M*, which includes his text 'You are the vine and we are the branches'.

Six Mainly Musicians

David V. Willcocks (b.1919): The King's organ scholar (1939–1940) returned in 1945 after an active army wartime, to become a Fellow until 1957, then Director of Music 1957-74. He has also held posts at Salisbury and Winchester Cathedrals and as Director of RCM. He made numerous broadcasts and recordings; one enduring legacy is the *Carols for Choirs* series launched with Reginald Jacques from 1961. Within congregational hymnals, his final-verse descants to 'Hark, the herald-angels sing', 'O come, all ye faithful' and 'Once in royal David's city' have become for many a vital ingredient of Christmas.[172] As well as several honorary doctorates he was awarded the CBE in 1971 and was knighted in 1977.

---

[171] Giles, Gordon, *Praying Thrice: Prayers from Hymns*, The Hymn Society of Great Britain and Ireland, Northwich, Cheshire, 2012
[172] For more on David Willcocks see Giles, Gordon, "Cambridge Carols".

Martin How (b.1931): Born in Liverpool, he studied Music and Theology at Clare, and after teaching in Grimsby became the RSCM's Southern Commissioner, frequently broadcasting with the Southern Cathedral Singers which he founded. One priority was training young choristers, which he did in Europe, the USA, South Africa and New Zealand; his tunes appear mainly in Anglican and Methodist books.

Derek W. Williams (1945-2006): This Sheffield-born and Sheffield-educated musician (head prefect at King Edward VII School) was organ scholar at Selwyn before joining the staff of the Cambridge University Library, where he was Head of the Music Department, 1970-89. He then became organist at the Anglican Shrine at Walsingham, Norfolk, where he died suddenly on New Year's Eve 2006. His best known hymn-tune is SAN ROCCO, composed in 1968 for Watts's 'Give me the wings of faith', but first published in the 1975 *New Church Praise* with Albert Bayly's 'Lord of the boundless curves of space.' *R&S* and the 2013 *A&M* are among the books using it for both texts, the latter adding a third since other contemporaries have found it ideal for their new words.

Andrew Wilson-Dickson (b.1946): A musicologist from London who studied at King's College, Cambridge (piano) then York (organ), he wrote *The Story of Christian Music*,[173] including many sections on hymns, now translated into a dozen languages. He has composed many tunes including more than thirty congregational Psalm settings. He moved to Cardiff to teach at the Royal Welsh College of Music and Drama and founded the Welsh Baroque Orchestra, which he leads from the harpsichord.

---

[173] Wilson-Dickson, Andrew, *The Story of Christian Music*, Lion Books, Oxford, 1992

Lindsay Gray (b.1953): After gaining his ARCO at school and graduating from King's where he was a counter-tenor choral scholar, he studied further at Durham and taught at Taunton and Cheltenham before spending fourteen years as Headmaster of Llandaff Cathedral School. He was Director of RSCM for five more years before returning to South Wales in 2012 as a consultant for music, education and charity development.

Andrew Reid (b.1971): On becoming RSCM's Director in 2012, he recalled that as a nine-year-old in Otford, Kent, he attended an RSCM training event and never looked back. A gifted organist even then, he studied music as organ scholar at St Catharine's, and later at Robinson College. He became organist at both Westminster Abbey and Westminster RC Cathedral, where he was impressed by Cardinal Basil Hume. He was then appointed Peterborough Cathedral's Director of Music until claimed by the RSCM. He aims to recapture true joy in worship, serve 'the silver generation' with lifelong learning, and promote hymns as integral to liturgy rather than fillers between other items.

Time Would Fail us to Tell ...

In some cases equally significant or effective, but for different reasons falling marginally outside the scope of this survey, are such Cambridge worthies as Frederick Barff, Gerard Brooks, Patrick Hadley, David McCarthy, Catherine Motyer Lowndes, Kenneth Naylor, Richard Shephard, and Peter G. White. The good news is that among today's so far little-known students are doubtless some who will make their mark among the hymns of tomorrow.

Even a glance through the above pages will reveal the African and North American connections; less surprising are the many links with Wales and Oxford, and the role of many in the HSGBI – secretaries, treasurers, chairmen and presidents, speakers, editors, presenters and committee members, conservationists and innovators, not to mention the immense range of activities well beyond the world of hymns, but which is perhaps insufficiently reflected in our Sunday singing.

Let that truly Oxbridge scholar, and far better our Lord of Nazareth, have the last word. Viewing the often unresolved tensions which arise wherever people sing God's praise, C.S. Lewis wrote that the most important thing Jesus ever said about hymns was to 'Love one another.'

Bibliography

KEY HYMNALS

100 Hymns for Today, William Clowes and Sons, London, 1969

Ancient & Modern: Hymns and Psalms for Refreshing Worship, Hymns Ancient & Modern Ltd, London, 2013

Anglican Hymn Book, Church Society / Oxford University Press, Oxford, 1965

Carol Praise, Peacock, David and Perry, Michael (Eds.), Marshall Pickering, London, 1987

Common Praise, Hymns Ancient & Modern Ltd., London, and Canterbury Press, Norwich, 2000

Hymns Ancient & Modern, Novello & Company, London, 1861; subsequent editions include:

Hymns Ancient & Modern Revised, William Clowes and Sons, London, 1950

Hymns Ancient & Modern New Standard, Hymns Ancient & Modern Ltd, London, 1983

Common Praise (2000), q.v.

Ancient & Modern: Hymns and Psalms for Refreshing Worship (2013), q.v.

Hymns and Psalms, Methodist Publishing House, London, 1983

Hymns and Songs, Methodist Publishing House, Peterborough, 1969

Hymns for Today's Church, Jubilate Hymns / Hodder & Stoughton, London, 1982; second edition, 1987

Mission Praise, Marshall Pickering / HarperCollins Religious, London, various editions from 1983 onwards

More Hymns for Today, William Clowes and Sons, London, 1980

New Church Praise, The United Reformed Church in England and Wales / Saint Andrew Press, Edinburgh, 1975

Praise! Psalms, Hymns and Songs for Christian Worship, Praise Trust, Darlington, 2000

Psalm Praise, Church Pastoral Aid Society / Falcon Books, London, 1973

Rejoice and Sing, Oxford University Press, Oxford, for the United Reformed Church, 1991

Sing Glory, Jubilate Hymns / Kevin Mayhew Ltd., Stowmarket, Suffolk, 1999

Sing Praise: Hymns and Songs for Refreshing Worship, Hymns Ancient & Modern Ltd. and the RSCM, London, 2012

Singing the Faith, Hymns Ancient & Modern Ltd., London, on behalf of the Trustees for Methodist Church Purposes, 2011

Songs of Worship, Scripture Union, Milton Keynes, 1980

The Baptist Hymn Book, Psalms and Hymns Trust, Didcot, 1962

The Cambridge Carol Book, Woodward, George Ratcliffe and Wood, Charles (Eds.), SPCK, London, 1924, reprinted 1951

The Cambridge Hymnal, Holbrook, David, and Poston, Elizabeth (Eds.), Cambridge University Press, London, 1967

The English Hymnal, Oxford University Press / A.R. Mowbray & Co., London, 1906

The New English Hymnal, English Hymnal Company / Canterbury Press, Norwich, 1986

Youth Praise, Baughen, Michael (Ed.), Church Pastoral Aid Society, Warwick: Book 1, 1966; Book 2, 1969

OTHER RESOURCES

The Canterbury Dictionary of Hymnology, – for extensive details of many hymn books, authors and hymns
http://www.hymnology.co.uk/

Index

"And whenne we hadde made an ende of our Visitatione of Cambridge, we hasted awaye withe all speede lest we sh^d suffere a Mischief."

From:

Babylon Bruis'd & Mount Moriah Mended; Being a compendious & authentick Narracioun of ye Proceedinges of ye Wm. Dowsing Societie in a Visitatione of all ye Parisshe Churches and College Chapells of Cambridge during a longe Vacation; wch Narration, latelie imprinted in ye Cambridge Review, is here newlie sett forth & edited by F. BRITTAIN & BERN^D MANNING, Fellows of Jesus College in ye Universitie of Cambridge.

Per quasdam vetustissimas et spissas valde horribilesque portas intravimus Babyloniam, Bernadus de Breydenbach, Itiner. Hiersosol

Cambridge: Printed & publish'd by Will. Heffer & Sons, & are to be hadde of divers booksellers. 1948.

The Hymn Society of Great Britain and Ireland was founded in 1936 and has four aims:

- Encouraging study and research in hymnody
- Promoting good standards of hymn-singing
- Encouraging the discerning use of hymns and songs in worship
- Sponsoring relevant publications

The Society is non-denominational and membership is open to all. Members receive a quarterly mailing which includes the Society's Bulletin and other documents. An annual conference lasting 2-3 days is held each summer and there are links with sister societies in North America and Europe. For further details see http://www.hymnsocietygbi.org.uk/

ISBN: 978-1-907018-08-4